MARÍA
AND ME

MARÍA

AND ME

A FATHER,
A DAUGHTER
(AND AUTISM)

MARÍA GALLARDO
MIGUEL GALLARDO

JKP

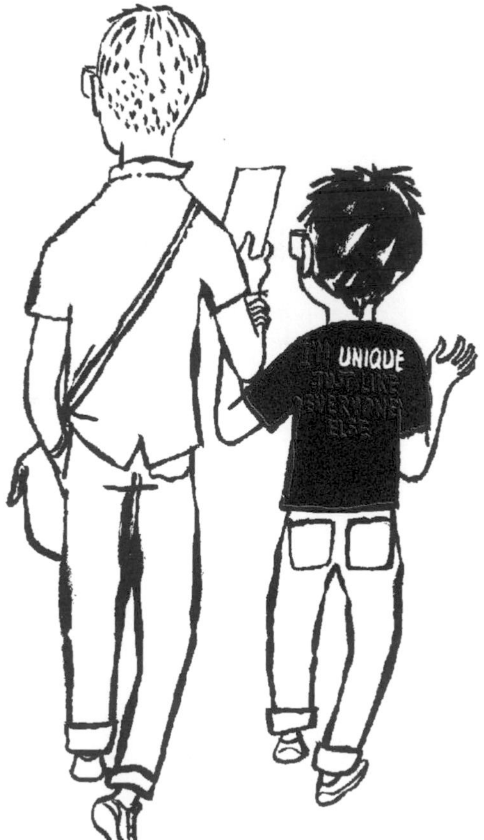
UNIQUE

FOR MAY AND
GRANDPA PEPE

MARÍA LIVES WITH HER MOTHER IN THE CANARY ISLANDS, A THREE-HOUR FLIGHT FROM BARCELONA, WHERE I LIVE. SOMETIMES WE GO ON VACATION TOGETHER FOR A WEEK TO A RESORT IN THE SOUTH OF GRAN CANARIA, WHICH IS VISITED BY GERMANS AND OTHER EUROPEAN TOURISTS. THIS IS THE STORY OF ONE SUCH TRIP, TRAVELING FROM BARCELONA TO TAKE ADVANTAGE OF THE FIRST DAYS OF SPRING IN ONE OF THOSE RESORT HOTELS. ON THESE TRIPS MARÍA AND I STUFF OURSELVES WITH FOOD, TALK, LAUGH AND MAKE LISTS OF PEOPLE.

MARÍA IS 12 YEARS OLD. SHE HAS AN INFECTIOUS SMILE AND A GREAT SENSE OF HUMOR. SHE ALSO HAS AUTISM.

FROM BARCELONA TO THE CANARIES

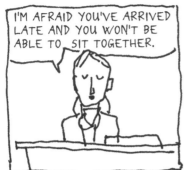

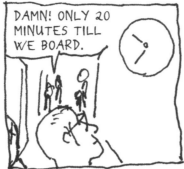

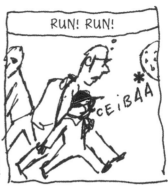

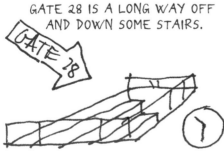

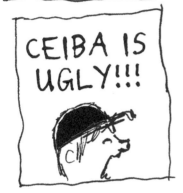

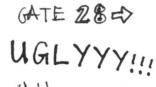

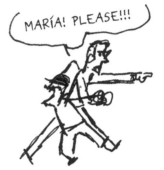

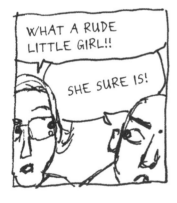

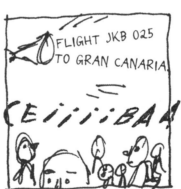

I'M AFRAID YOU'VE ARRIVED LATE AND YOU WON'T BE ABLE TO SIT TOGETHER.
DAMN! ONLY 20 MINUTES TILL WE BOARD.
RUN! RUN!
CEIBAA*
CEIBA IS UGLY!!!
GATE 28 ⇨
UGLYYY!!!
MARÍA! PLEASE!!!
WHAT A RUDE LITTLE GIRL!!
SHE SURE IS!
FLIGHT JKB 025 TO GRAN CANARIA
CEiiiiiBAA
TIME GOES BY.
GATE 28 IS A LONG WAY OFF AND DOWN SOME STAIRS.
GATE 28
AT LAST WE SIT DOWN, BUT THAT STILL DOESN'T CALM MARÍA.
CEIBAAAAA

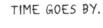

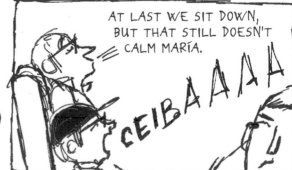

* CEIBA IS ONE OF MARÍA'S FAVORITE CANARIAN COUSINS.

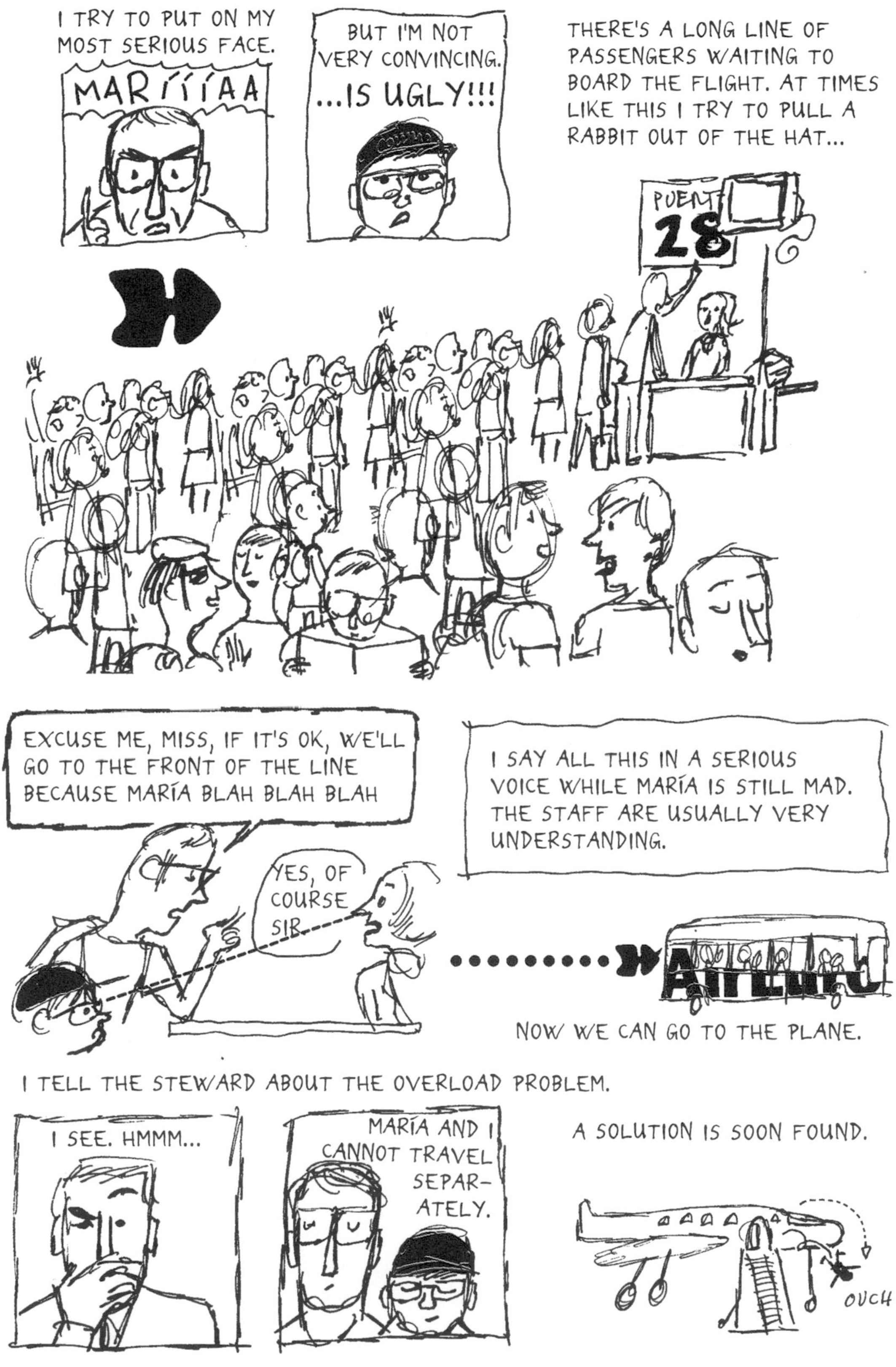
I TRY TO PUT ON MY MOST SERIOUS FACE.
MARÍÍÍAA
BUT I'M NOT VERY CONVINCING.
...IS UGLY!!!
THERE'S A LONG LINE OF PASSENGERS WAITING TO BOARD THE FLIGHT. AT TIMES LIKE THIS I TRY TO PULL A RABBIT OUT OF THE HAT...
PUENT
28
EXCUSE ME, MISS, IF IT'S OK, WE'LL GO TO THE FRONT OF THE LINE BECAUSE MARÍA BLAH BLAH BLAH
YES, OF COURSE SIR
I SAY ALL THIS IN A SERIOUS VOICE WHILE MARÍA IS STILL MAD. THE STAFF ARE USUALLY VERY UNDERSTANDING.
NOW WE CAN GO TO THE PLANE.
I TELL THE STEWARD ABOUT THE OVERLOAD PROBLEM.
I SEE. HMMM...
MARÍA AND I CANNOT TRAVEL SEPAR-ATELY.
A SOLUTION IS SOON FOUND.
OUCH

PARANOIA/TURBULENCE

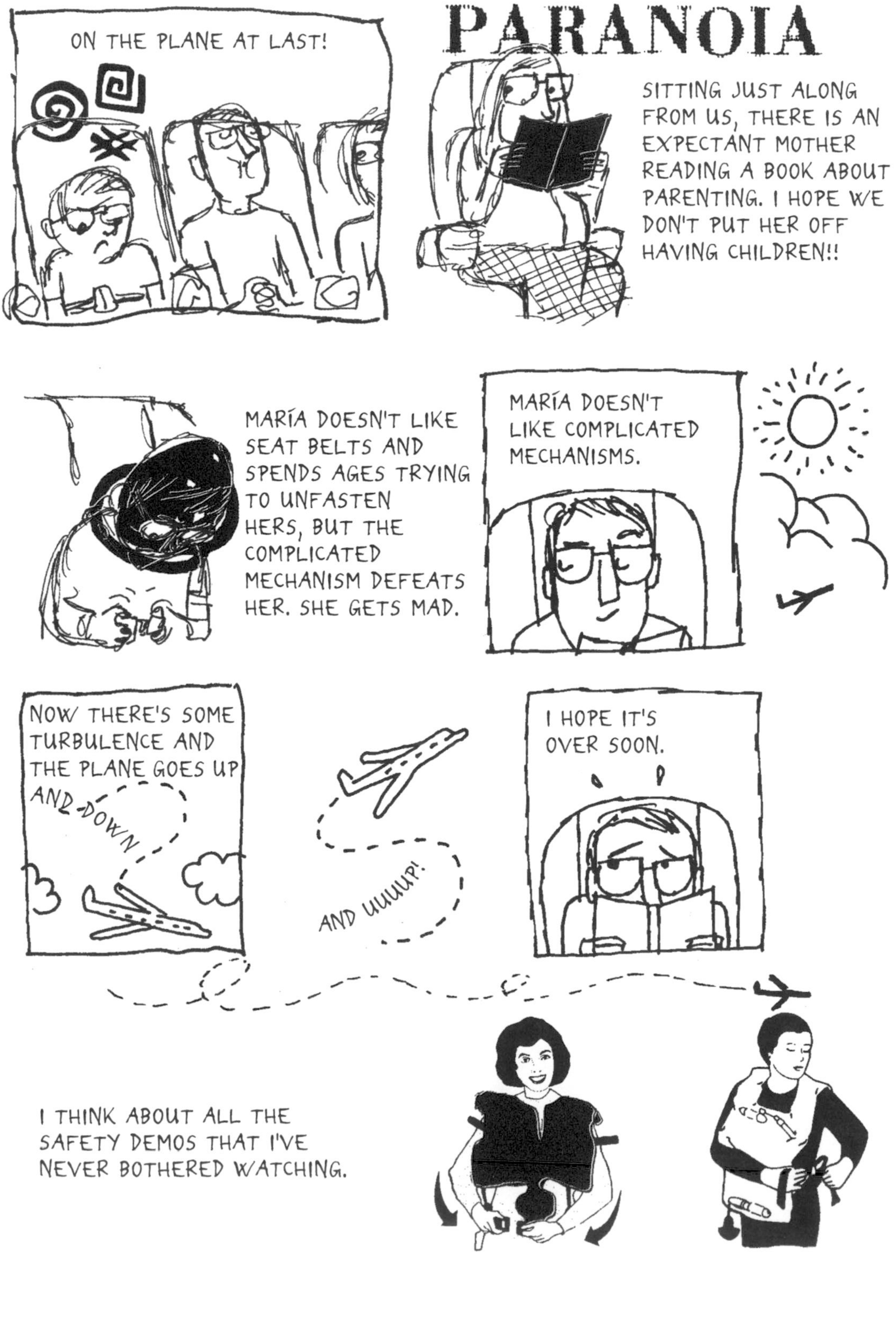

ON THE PLANE AT LAST!
PARANOIA
SITTING JUST ALONG FROM US, THERE IS AN EXPECTANT MOTHER READING A BOOK ABOUT PARENTING. I HOPE WE DON'T PUT HER OFF HAVING CHILDREN!!
MARÍA DOESN'T LIKE SEAT BELTS AND SPENDS AGES TRYING TO UNFASTEN HERS, BUT THE COMPLICATED MECHANISM DEFEATS HER. SHE GETS MAD.
MARÍA DOESN'T LIKE COMPLICATED MECHANISMS.
NOW THERE'S SOME TURBULENCE AND THE PLANE GOES UP
AND DOWN
AND UUUUP!
I HOPE IT'S OVER SOON.
I THINK ABOUT ALL THE SAFETY DEMOS THAT I'VE NEVER BOTHERED WATCHING.

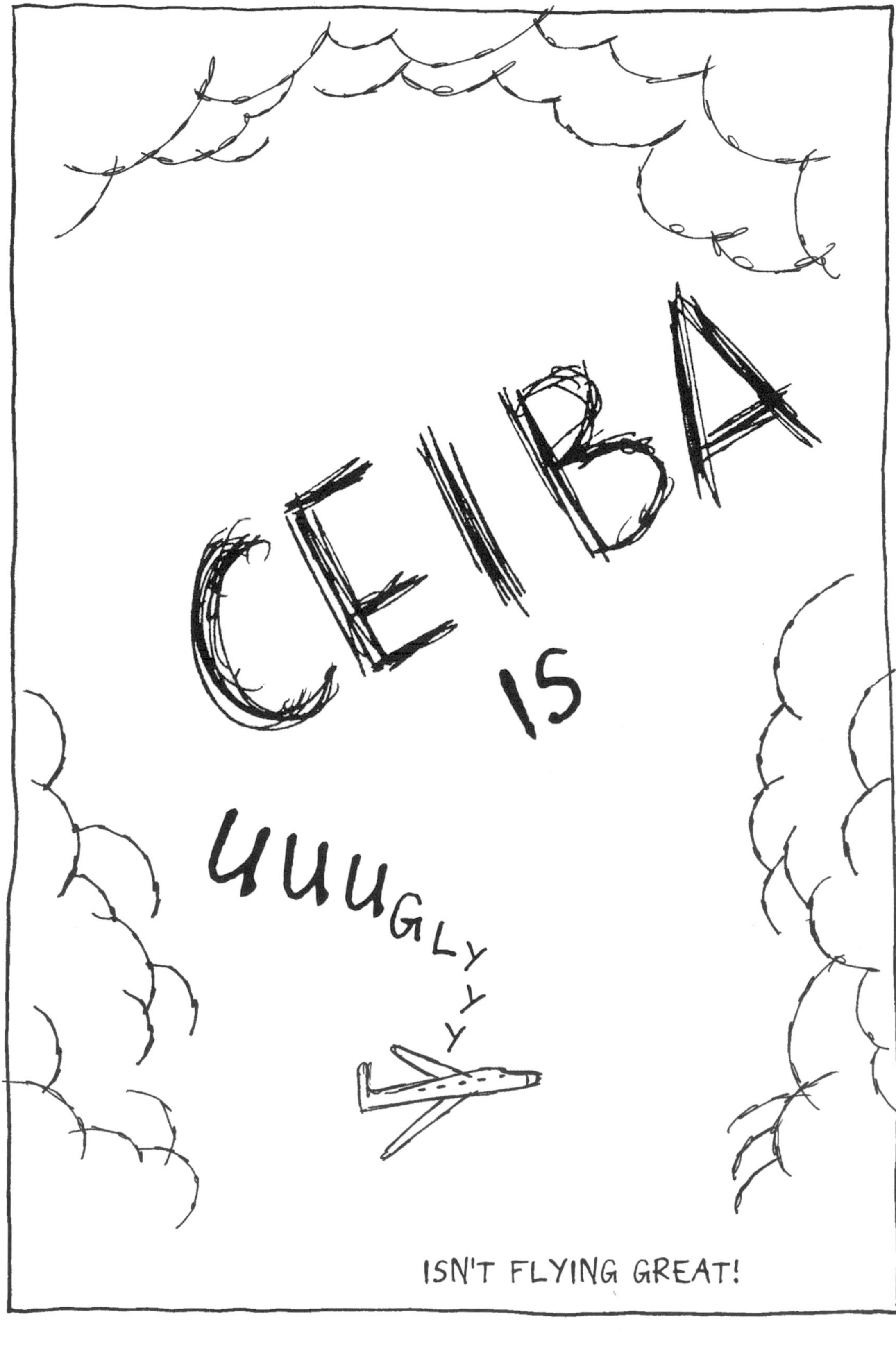
CEIBA
IS
UUUGLYYYY
ISN'T FLYING GREAT!

ARRIVAL

WE'VE ARRIVED FROM BARCELONA, WHERE IT WAS GRAY AND GLOOMY, AND NOW WE'RE IN THIS PARADISE OF 365 DAYS GUARANTEED SUNSHINE.

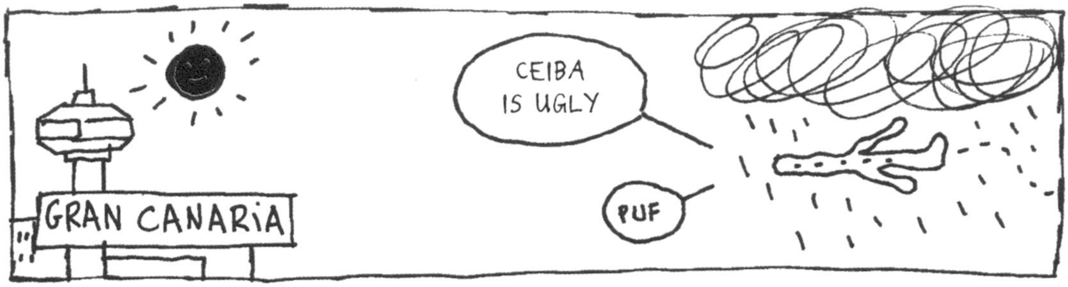
GRAN CANARIA
CEIBA IS UGLY
PUF

MARÍA IS HAPPY WE'VE ARRIVED AND SHOWS IT IN HER OWN WAY.

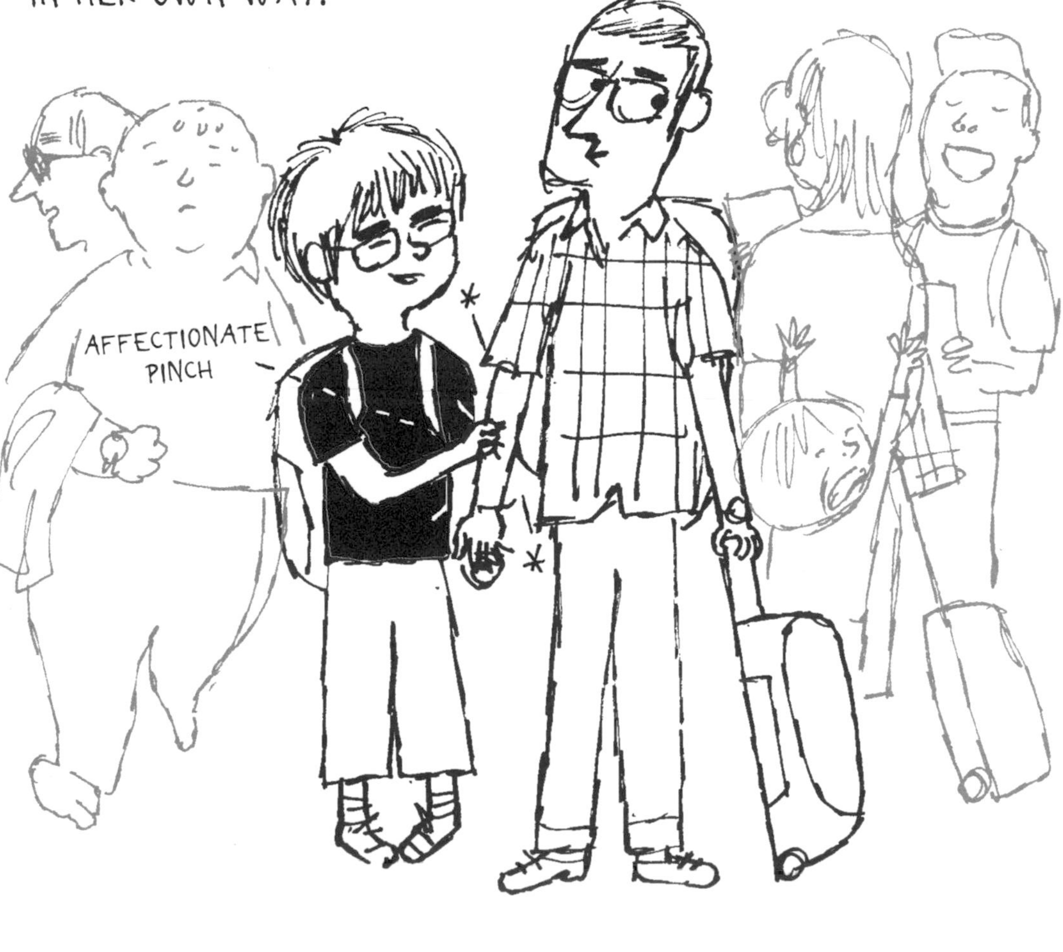
AFFECTIONATE PINCH

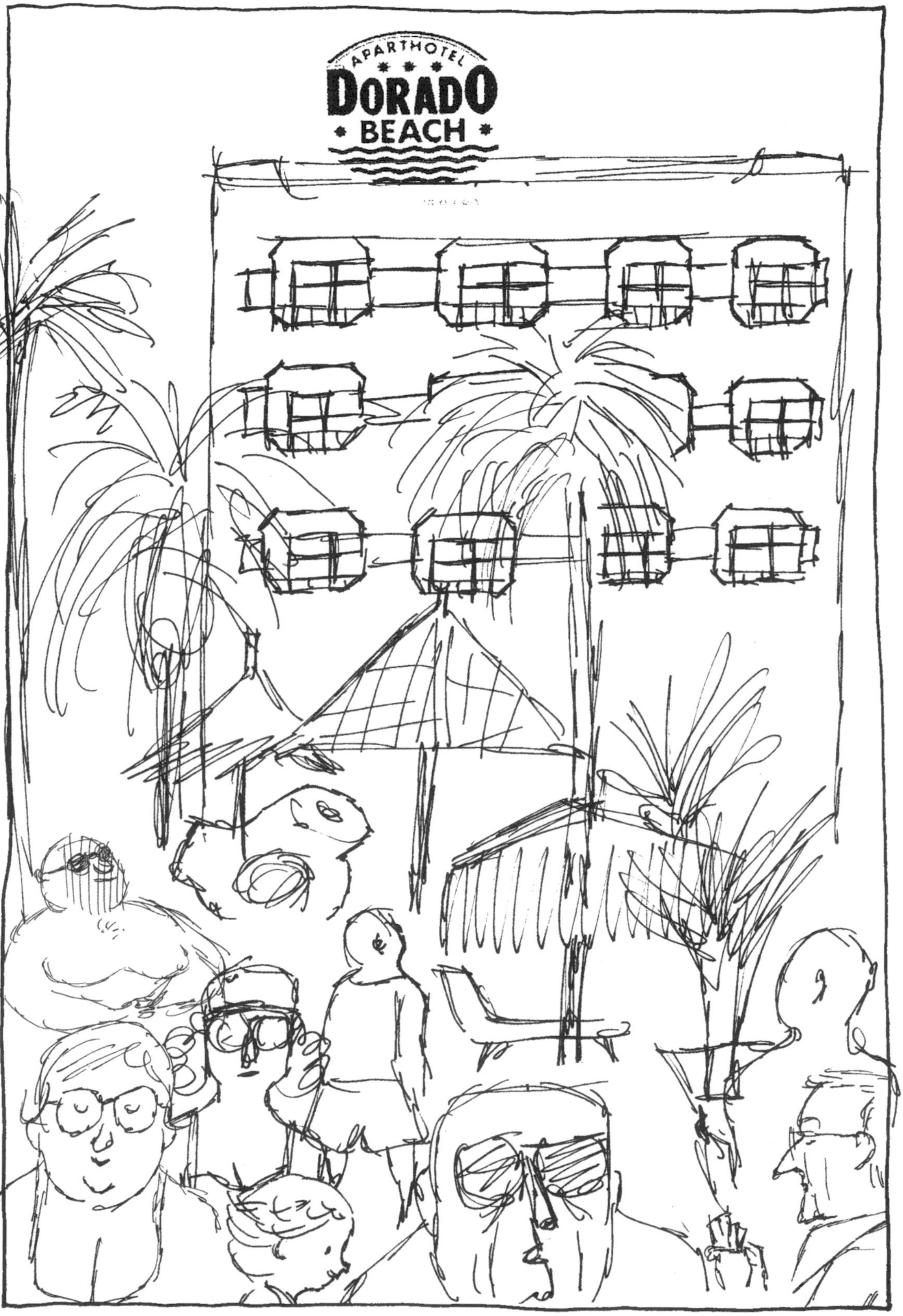
APARTHOTEL
DORADO
BEACH

THE DORADO BEACH HOTEL

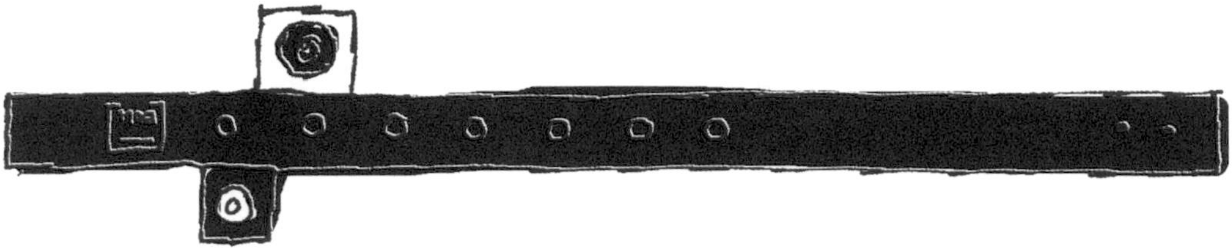

I WEAR A RED BRACELET, WHICH MEANS THAT I CAN DRINK WHATEVER I LIKE THROUGHOUT THE WHOLE BEAUTIFUL RESORT – EVEN, I IMAGINE, AT THE FABULOUS KARAOKE EVENING THAT TAKES PLACE EVERY WEDNESDAY IN THE SUNBEACH LOUNGE. MARÍA ALSO HAS A BRACELET, BUT HERS IS GREEN, WHICH MEANS THAT, UNLIKE ME, SHE CAN'T HAVE A DAIQUIRI IN THE MIDDLE OF THE AFTERNOON.

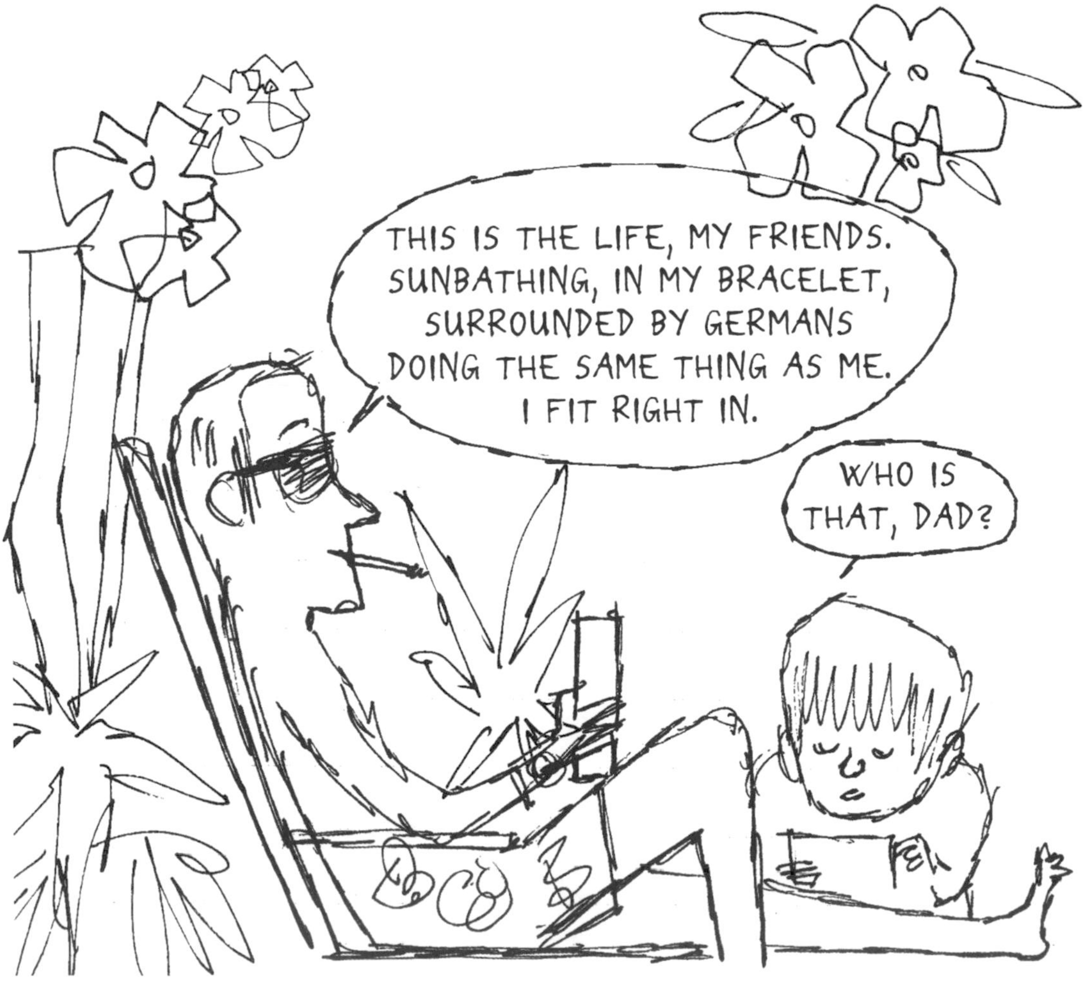
THIS IS THE LIFE, MY FRIENDS. SUNBATHING, IN MY BRACELET, SURROUNDED BY GERMANS DOING THE SAME THING AS ME. I FIT RIGHT IN.
WHO IS THAT, DAD?

THE DORADO BEACH IS A SANCTUARY FOR GERMANS. ARMED WITH THEIR RED BRACELETS, THEY CAN WANDER AROUND THE RESORT WITHOUT WORRYING ABOUT THE NATIVES.

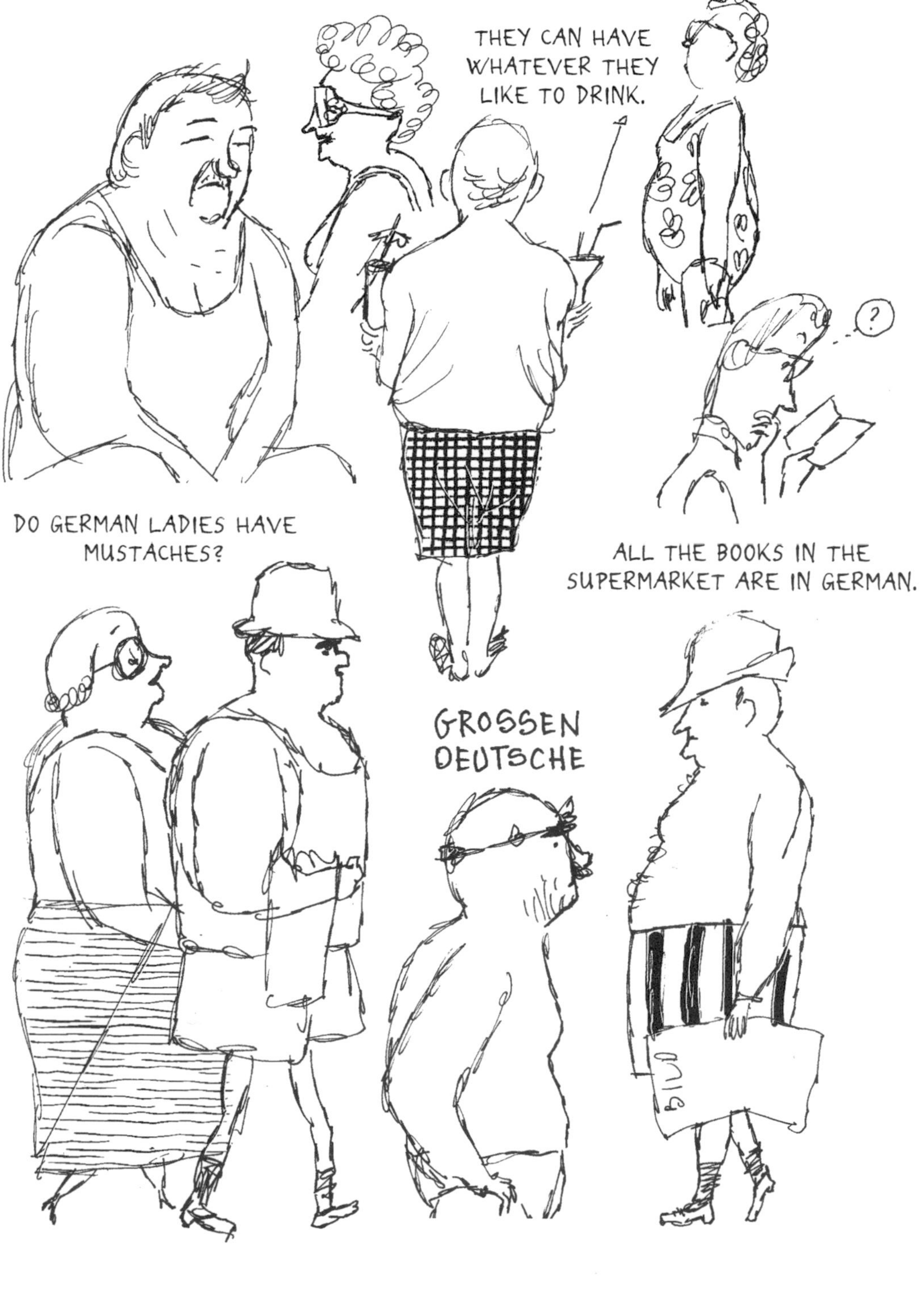
THEY CAN HAVE WHATEVER THEY LIKE TO DRINK.
?
DO GERMAN LADIES HAVE MUSTACHES?
ALL THE BOOKS IN THE SUPERMARKET ARE IN GERMAN.
GROSSEN DEUTSCHE

THEIR NATURAL HABITAT IS THE HOTEL POOL, WHERE THEY CONGREGATE RELIGIOUSLY EVERY DAY TO SUNBATHE AND ACQUIRE THEIR TYPICAL LOBSTER COLORING. GROUPS OF THEM CAN ALSO BE SEEN AT THE ALL-YOU-CAN-EAT BUFFET.

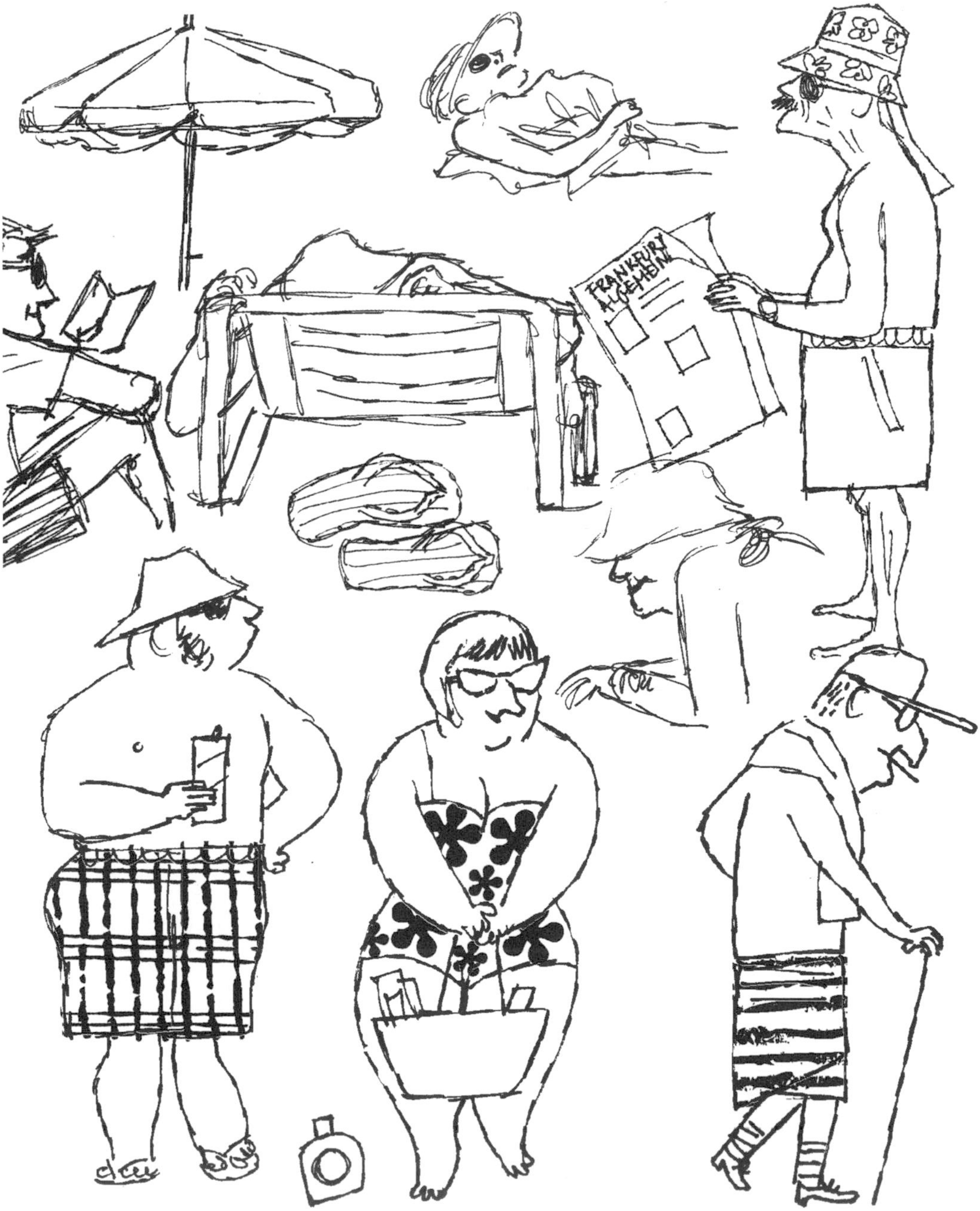
FRANKFURT

THE BUFFET IS ONE OF THE HIGHLIGHTS OF THE HOTEL, ALONG WITH THE DARTS CHAMPIONSHIPS AND THE AQUAGYM SESSIONS.

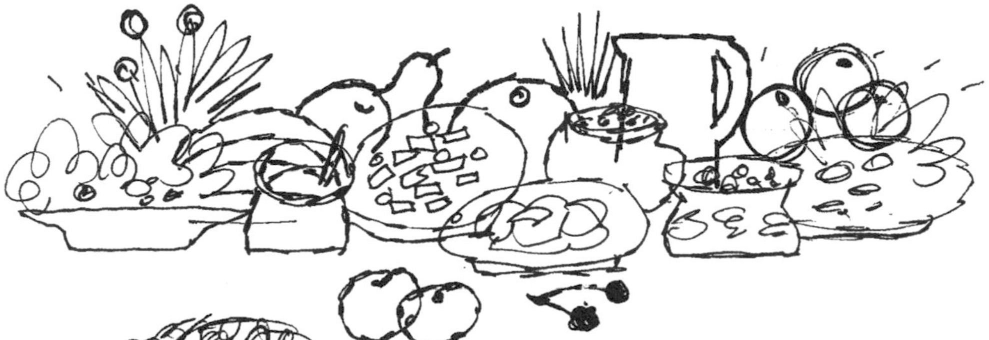

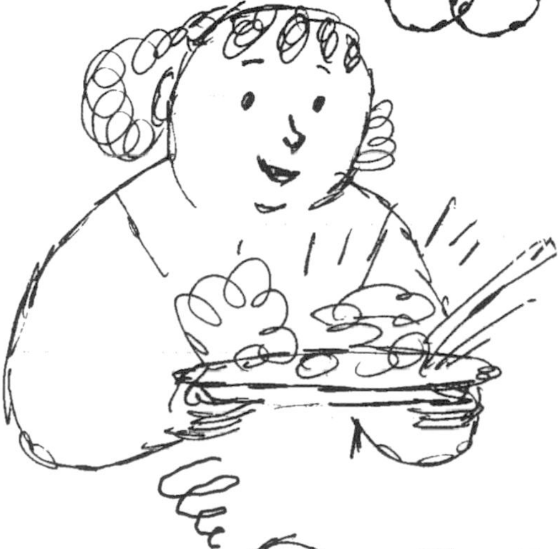

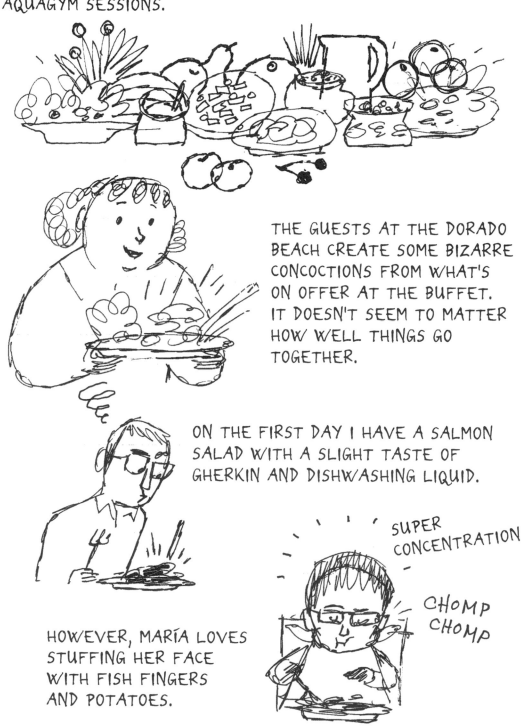

THE GUESTS AT THE DORADO BEACH CREATE SOME BIZARRE CONCOCTIONS FROM WHAT'S ON OFFER AT THE BUFFET. IT DOESN'T SEEM TO MATTER HOW WELL THINGS GO TOGETHER.

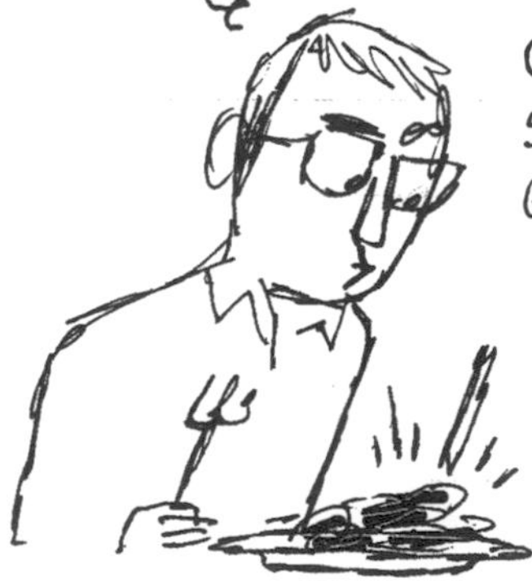

ON THE FIRST DAY I HAVE A SALMON SALAD WITH A SLIGHT TASTE OF GHERKIN AND DISHWASHING LIQUID.

HOWEVER, MARÍA LOVES STUFFING HER FACE WITH FISH FINGERS AND POTATOES.

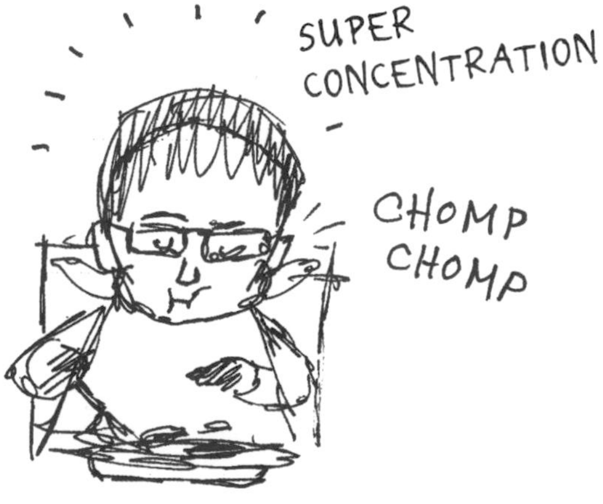
SUPER CONCENTRATION
CHOMP CHOMP

MARÍA

DRAWINGS

ONE OF THE THINGS THAT MARÍA ENJOYS MOST IS ME DRAWING THE PEOPLE SHE KNOWS. THIS TIME I'VE COME PREPARED. AS WELL AS MY SKETCHPAD, I'VE BROUGHT A LAMINATED SET OF DRAWINGS OF ALL HER FRIENDS AND RELATIVES. SHE LOVES TO POINT OUT AND NAME EVERYONE.

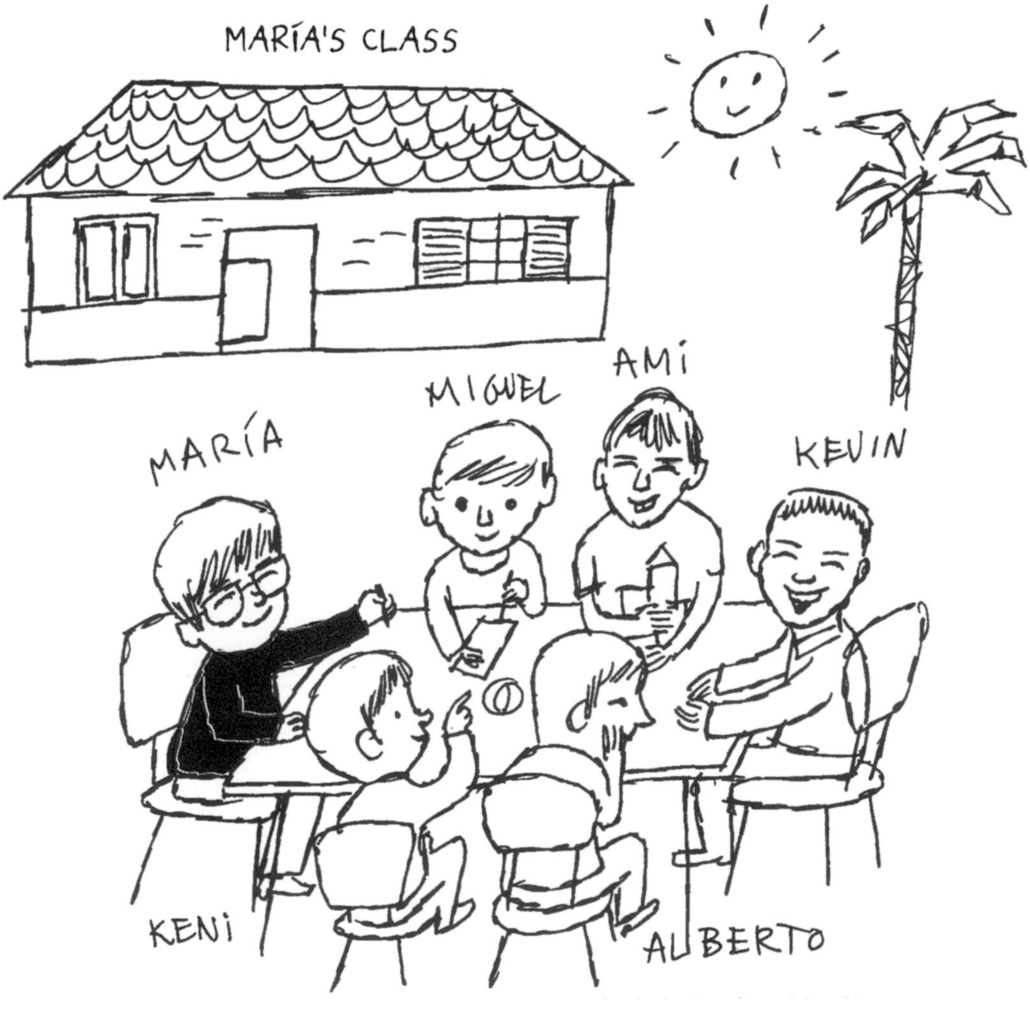
MARÍA'S CLASS
AMI
MIGUEL
MARÍA
KEVIN
KENI
ALBERTO

THESE ARE HER CLASSMATES AT SCHOOL IN THE CANARY ISLANDS, WHERE SHE'S THE ONLY PRINCESS SURROUNDED BY THE BOYS. HER FAVORITE GAME IS TO REPEAT OVER AND OVER THE LINE-UP OF HER OWN PERSONAL TEAMS: CLASSMATES, TEACHERS, UNCLES AND AUNTS, COUSINS AND SO ON.

FACES

MARÍA'S INFECTIOUS LAUGH LIGHTS UP THE WHOLE ROOM.

AT FIRST, YOU MIGHT ASSUME THAT NOT MUCH INTERESTS MARÍA, BUT I THINK THAT'S BECAUSE WE DON'T UNDERSTAND HER.

BY REPEATING THE NAMES OF ALL THE PEOPLE SHE'S MET (INCLUDING THOSE WHO ARE NO LONGER AROUND), MARÍA IS ABLE TO REASSURE HERSELF THAT EVERYTHING IS IN ORDER AND THE WORLD IS A SAFE PLACE. I OFTEN LACK THIS BLIND FAITH THAT SHE HAS IN PEOPLE.

FACES I DON'T LIKE TO SEE WHEN PEOPLE LOOK AT MARÍA

THESE ARE THE FACES THAT PEOPLE MAKE WHEN, FOR EXAMPLE, MARÍA MAKES A SCENE IN A RESTAURANT BECAUSE SHE'S NERVOUS OR BECAUSE I TELL HER NOT TO EAT SO FAST. THESE FACES MAKE ME SAD AND SOMETIMES ANNOY ME.

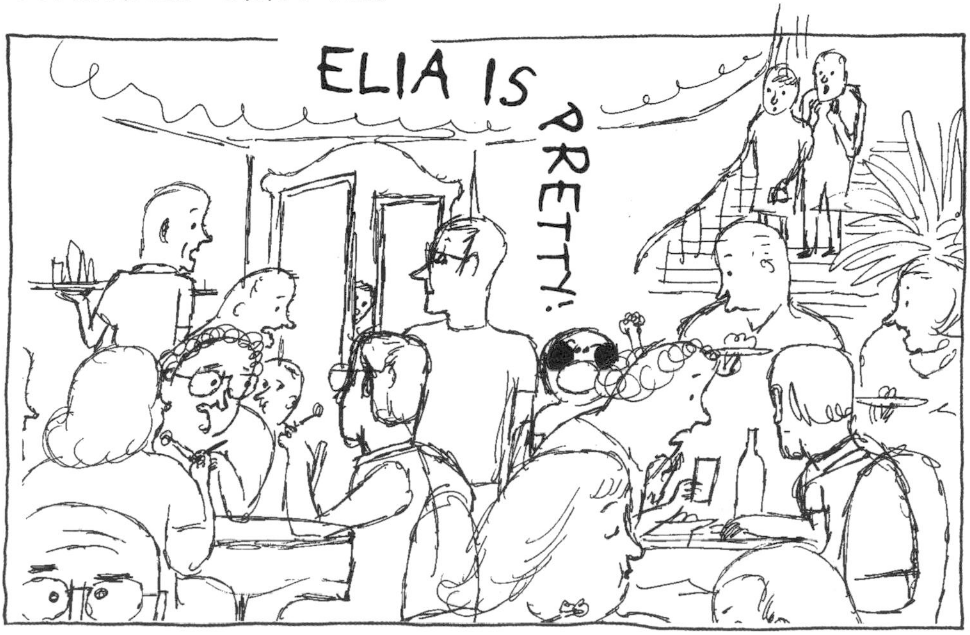
ELIA IS PRETTY!

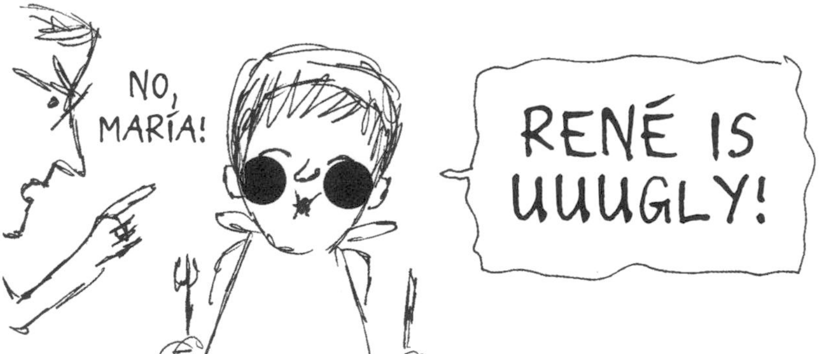
NO, MARÍA!
RENÉ IS UUUGLY!

SOMETIMES I'D LIKE TO TELL THEM, TOO:

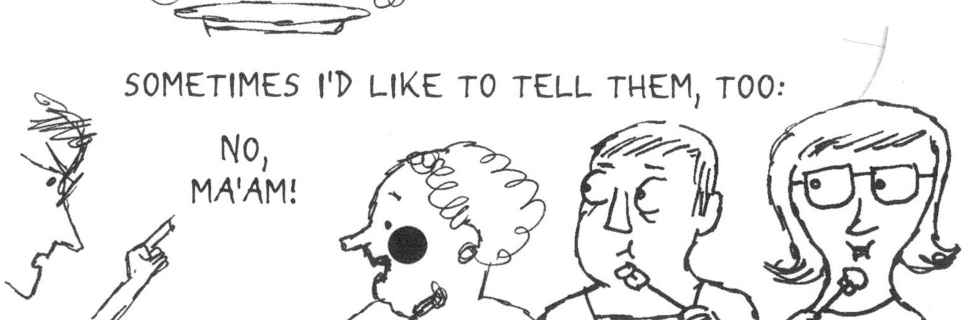
NO, MA'AM!

UNIQUE

THE OTHER DAY, AMONG THE T-SHIRTS THAT MARÍA'S MOTHER HAD PACKED FOR HER, THERE WAS ONE THAT SEEMED IDEAL FOR THE SITUATION:

RED COTTON

I'M UNIQUE JUST LIKE EVERYONE ELSE

IMPOSSIBLE NOT TO NOTICE!

SHINY LETTERS!

I PUT IT ON HER SO THAT SHE'D BE THE QUEEN OF THE DINING ROOM, BUT I DON'T THINK ANYONE GOT THE MESSAGE. THAT'S THE THING ABOUT MARÍA: SHE IS THE STAR, NOT THE T-SHIRTS SHE WEARS.

EVERYTHING IS FALLING INTO PLACE

I THINK OF THIS SONG BY KEVIN JOHANSEN WHEN I SEE MARÍA ON THE BEACH PLAYING WITH THE SAND. FOR HOURS ON END, SHE LETS THE GRAINS SLIP THROUGH HER HAND, RIGHT IN FRONT OF HER EYES, AS IF SHE CAN SEE THE THING THAT WE ARE ALL DESPERATELY LOOKING FOR.

THIS IS ONE OF MARÍA'S FAVORITE RITUALS. SHE'S DONE IT SINCE SHE WAS VERY SMALL.

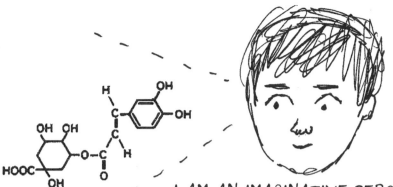

I AM AN IMAGINATIVE PERSON AND I FANTASIZE THAT MARÍA CAN SEE THE COMPOSITION OF ATOMS, OR MAYBE SEE NEW WORLDS OR STARS...OR MAYBE JUST FALLING SAND. BUT MARÍA IS HAPPY WHEN THE SAND IS PASSING THROUGH HER FINGERS. WATCHING GRAINS OF SAND FALL FOR HOURS AND HOURS...LIKE A CLOCK SLOWLY TICKING. EVERYTHING IS FALLING INTO PLACE.

SOMETIMES SHE PAUSES HER GAME TO MAKE AN IMPORTANT ANNOUNCEMENT. I THINK SHE DOES THIS JUST TO LET US KNOW THAT SHE'S STILL THERE.

RENÉ HAS A HORSE
LETI GOT MAD
CEIBA PINCHED ME!
MARTITA GOT INTO TROUBLE
KEVIN'S MOM CAME

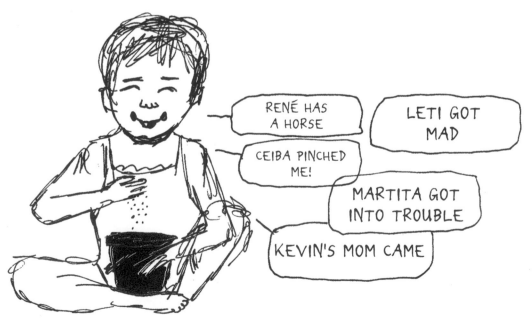

COMIC INTERLUDE

AFTER THROWING A BALL AT ME ON THE BEACH, AN ISLANDER TOOK ME FOR A FOREIGNER AND SAID "SORRY" IN ENGLISH. JUST LIKE THAT, I PASSED FROM "GODO" ✱ TO "PENINSULAR"✱ TO FOREIGNER. MY RECENTLY ACQUIRED LOBSTER COLORING GRANTS ME THE SAME STATUS AS MY FELLOW GUESTS AT THE DORADO BEACH. I MUST LEARN SOME GERMAN AND THEN I'LL REALLY FIT IN!

NOW MARÍA IS ASLEEP.

SHE HAS FALLEN ASLEEP HUGGING HER PILLOW AS USUAL.

AFTER OUR MORNING WALK, THE HOTEL BREAKFAST, THREE HOURS AT THE POOL, LUNCH, THE JOURNEY TO THE BEACH, FOUR HOURS OF SAND PLAY AT THE BEACH, A WALK ROUND THE TOWN TO BUILD UP AN APPETITE AND THEN THE BUFFET, MARÍA HAS RUN OUT OF BATTERY. I HAVE TOO!

✱ GODO: PEJORATIVE CANARIAN TERM FOR A SPANISH TOURIST.
   PENINSULAR: SOMEWHAT BETTER...AN ACCEPTABLE SPANISH MAINLANDER.

LISTS

TODAY'S LISTS OF PEOPLE HAVE BEEN LIKE QUESTIONS IN A TV SHOW WHERE I HAVE TO GUESS WHO MARÍA IS TALKING ABOUT. THEY COULD BE THE KIDS FROM HER CLASS (I ALREADY KNOW WHO THEY ARE) OR THEY COULD BE THE KIDS WHO WENT TO CAMP, OR THOSE AT THE WATER FESTIVAL...AS WELL AS THEIR MOTHERS' FULL NAMES.

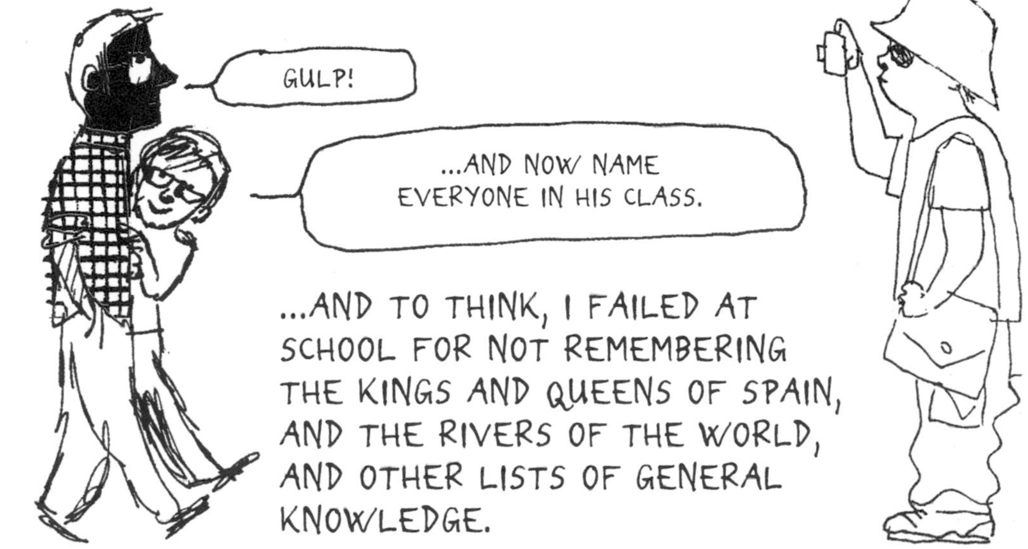
GULP!
...AND NOW NAME EVERYONE IN HIS CLASS.

...AND TO THINK, I FAILED AT SCHOOL FOR NOT REMEMBERING THE KINGS AND QUEENS OF SPAIN, AND THE RIVERS OF THE WORLD, AND OTHER LISTS OF GENERAL KNOWLEDGE.

EVERY MORNING, ALTHOUGH IT'S STRICTLY FORBIDDEN, THE GUESTS IN THE HOTEL PUT THEIR TOWELS ON THE SUN LOUNGERS TO SAVE THEIR SPOT. IT'S LIKE A SMALL INVESTMENT IN THE FUTURE: LET NOBODY TAKE AWAY OUR PLACE IN THE SUN!

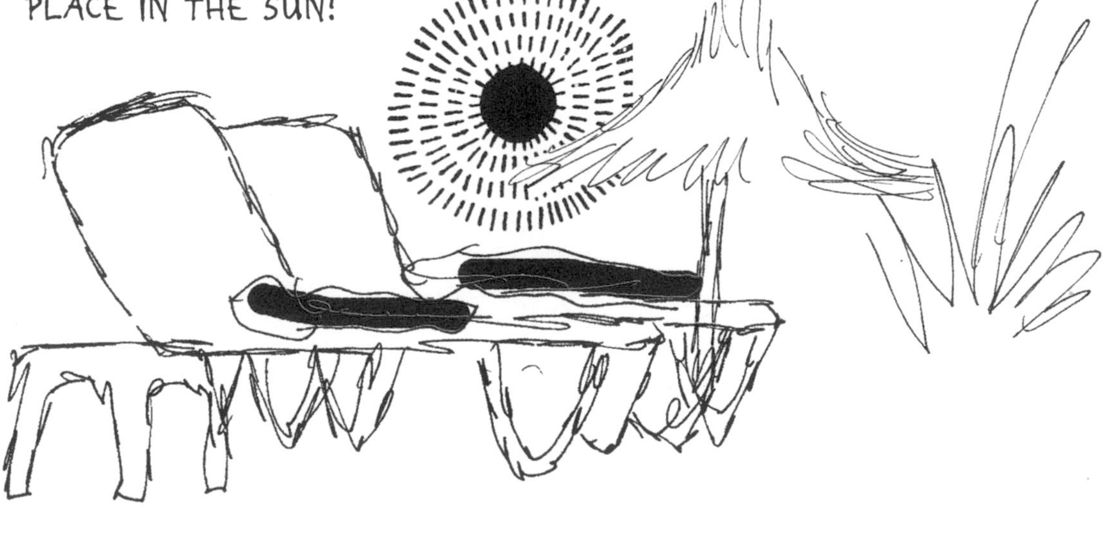

AT THE BEGINNING OF EVERY DAY IN THIS SECOND-RATE REFUGEE CAMP, THE PUBLIC ADDRESS SYSTEM COMES TO LIFE WITH STATIC INTERFERENCE.
KKKKRR...LADIES AND GENTLEMEN, WELCOME...KKKKKRR

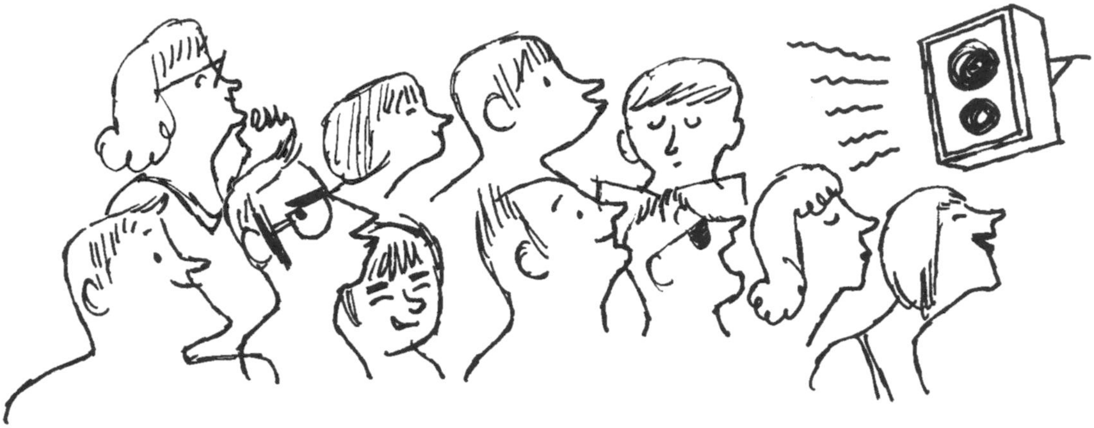

MORE STATIC NOISE. EVERYONE STOPS TO LISTEN.
TODAY AT 12 NOON, THE WATERPOLO CHAMPIONSHIP...
(THE SAME MESSAGE IN GERMAN)...SILENCE...
ANYONE FOR WATERPOLO?
EMBARRASSED SILENCE...STATIC NOISE AGAIN.
ADULT AND CHILDREN'S DARTS COMPETITION
LONG SILENCE...ANYONE FOR DARTS?
NOBODY GETS UP. THE GERMAN NATIONAL TEAM IS EXHAUSTED AFTER A NIGHT OF KARAOKE.
TIME FOR ANOTHER DAIQUIRI!

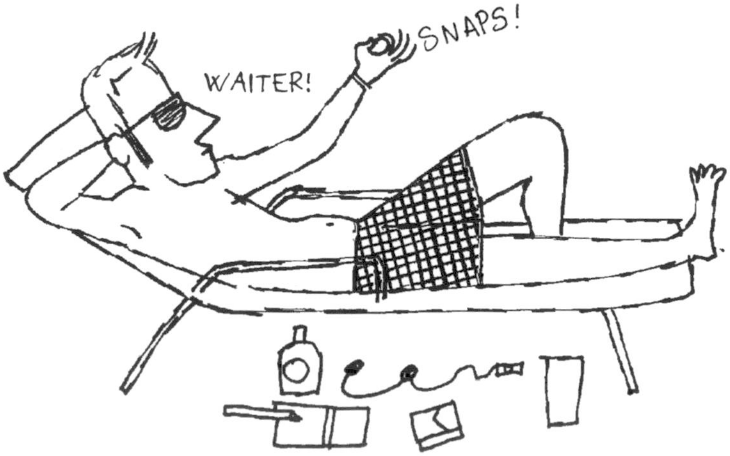
WAITER!
SNAPS!

ME   MARÍA

AS WELL AS STRONG, THICK HAIR — MINE WHITE, HERS BLACK — MARÍA HAS ALSO INHERITED THE FAMILY NOSE AND A ROUND FACE, WITH HER MOTHER'S DIMPLES. WE ALSO SHARE CERTAIN PECULIARITIES AND HABITS — MINE I HAVE INVENTED, AND HERS ARE A MIXTURE OF HER AUTISM AND BEING STUBBORN LIKE HER GRANDMOTHER. WE ARE BOTH RELUCTANT TO CHANGE AND WE WANT EVERYTHING TO BE IN ITS PLACE.

FOOD

WALKS · POOL · CANARIES

PHOTOS · BARCELONA · FRIENDS

SAND · NAMES · SWIMMING

QUESTIONS · BIRTHDAYS · OTHER STUFF

ITINERARIES

WHEN MARÍA AND I MEET UP SOMEWHERE IN THE CANARY ISLANDS OR IN BARCELONA, WE MAKE UP RITUALS AND ITINERARIES THAT WE'RE BOTH HAPPY WITH (IN CASE I HAVEN'T ALREADY SAID THIS, ONCE SOMETHING'S BEEN DECIDED UPON, MARÍA DOESN'T LIKE CHANGES TO THE SCHEDULE). FOR EXAMPLE:

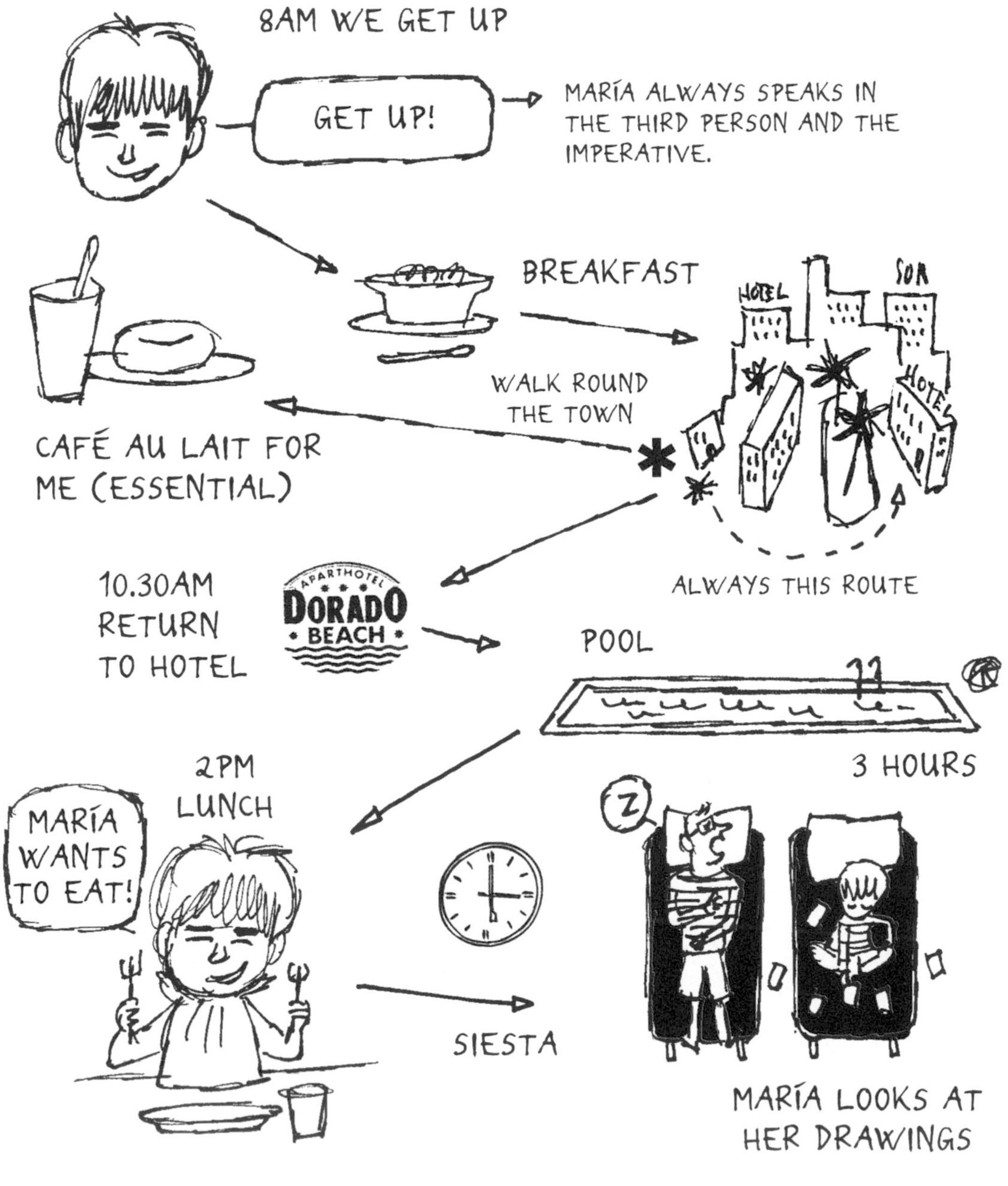
8AM WE GET UP
GET UP!
MARÍA ALWAYS SPEAKS IN THE THIRD PERSON AND THE IMPERATIVE.
BREAKFAST
CAFÉ AU LAIT FOR ME (ESSENTIAL)
HOTEL
SOR
HOTEL
WALK ROUND THE TOWN
ALWAYS THIS ROUTE
10.30AM RETURN TO HOTEL
APARTHOTEL
DORADO
BEACH
POOL
3 HOURS
2PM LUNCH
MARÍA WANTS TO EAT!
SIESTA
MARÍA LOOKS AT HER DRAWINGS

ALL THIS IN PREPARATION FOR THE HIGHLIGHT OF THE DAY:

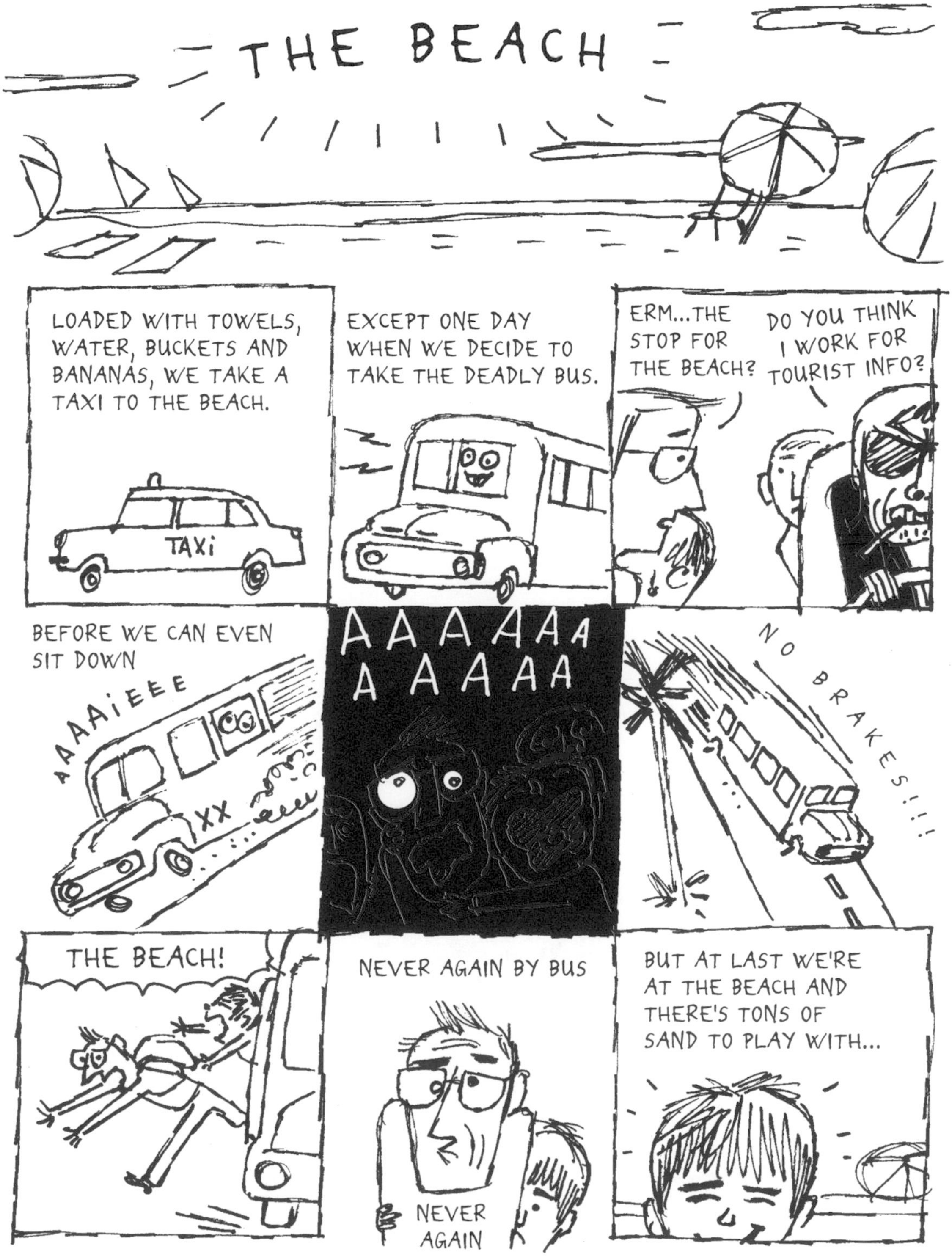
THE BEACH
LOADED WITH TOWELS, WATER, BUCKETS AND BANANAS, WE TAKE A TAXI TO THE BEACH.
TAXI
EXCEPT ONE DAY WHEN WE DECIDE TO TAKE THE DEADLY BUS.
ERM...THE STOP FOR THE BEACH?
DO YOU THINK I WORK FOR TOURIST INFO?
BEFORE WE CAN EVEN SIT DOWN
AAAAiEEE
XX
AAAAAA
AAAAA
NO BRAKES!!!
THE BEACH!
NEVER AGAIN BY BUS
NEVER AGAIN
BUT AT LAST WE'RE AT THE BEACH AND THERE'S TONS OF SAND TO PLAY WITH...

AND AGAIN THERE ARE THOSE LOOKS. ALWAYS THOSE LOOKS.

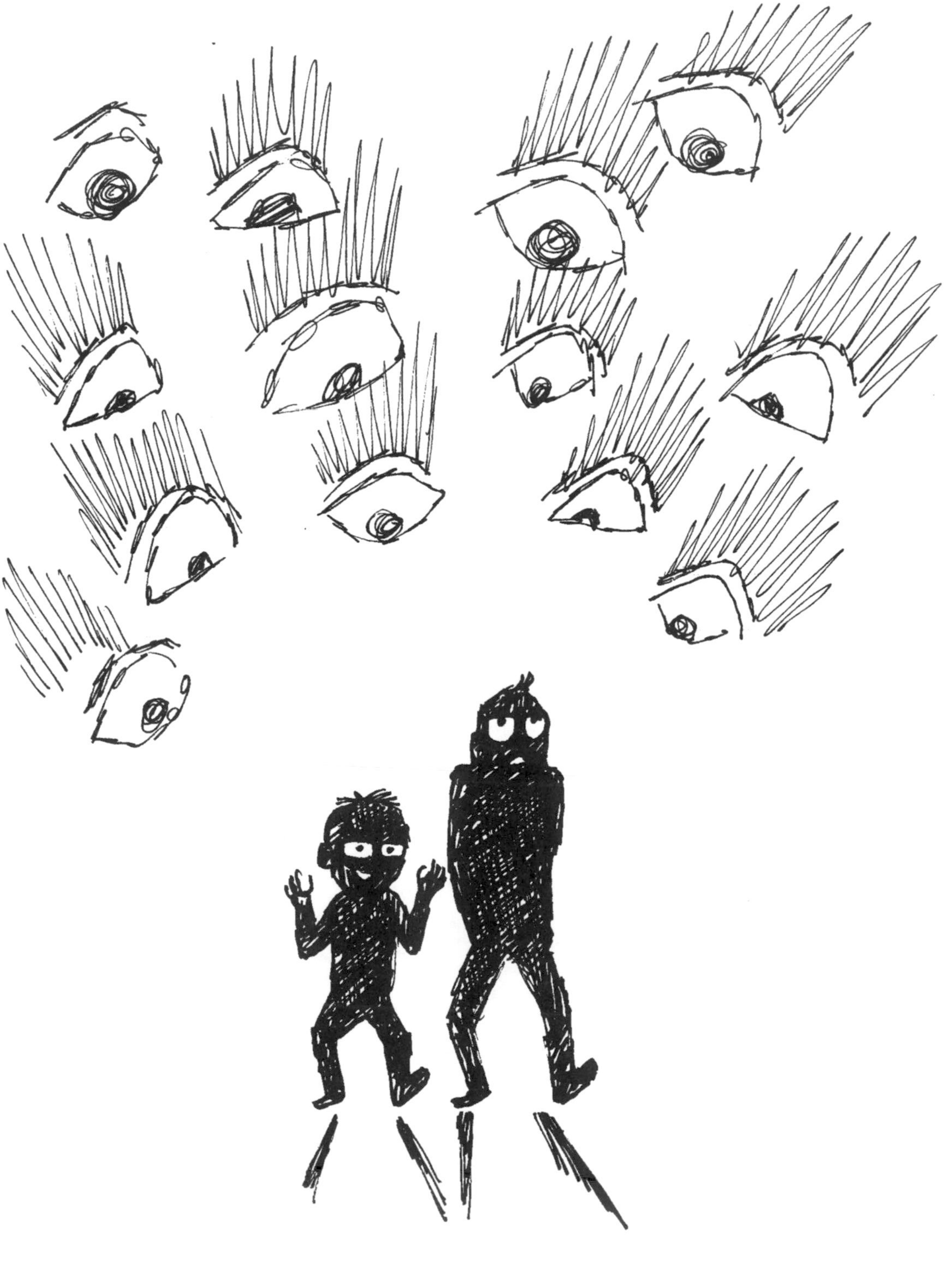

ANYWAY! ... IT'S PARTY TIME AT THE DORADO BEACH!
ANOTHER WONDERFUL SUNNY DAY!

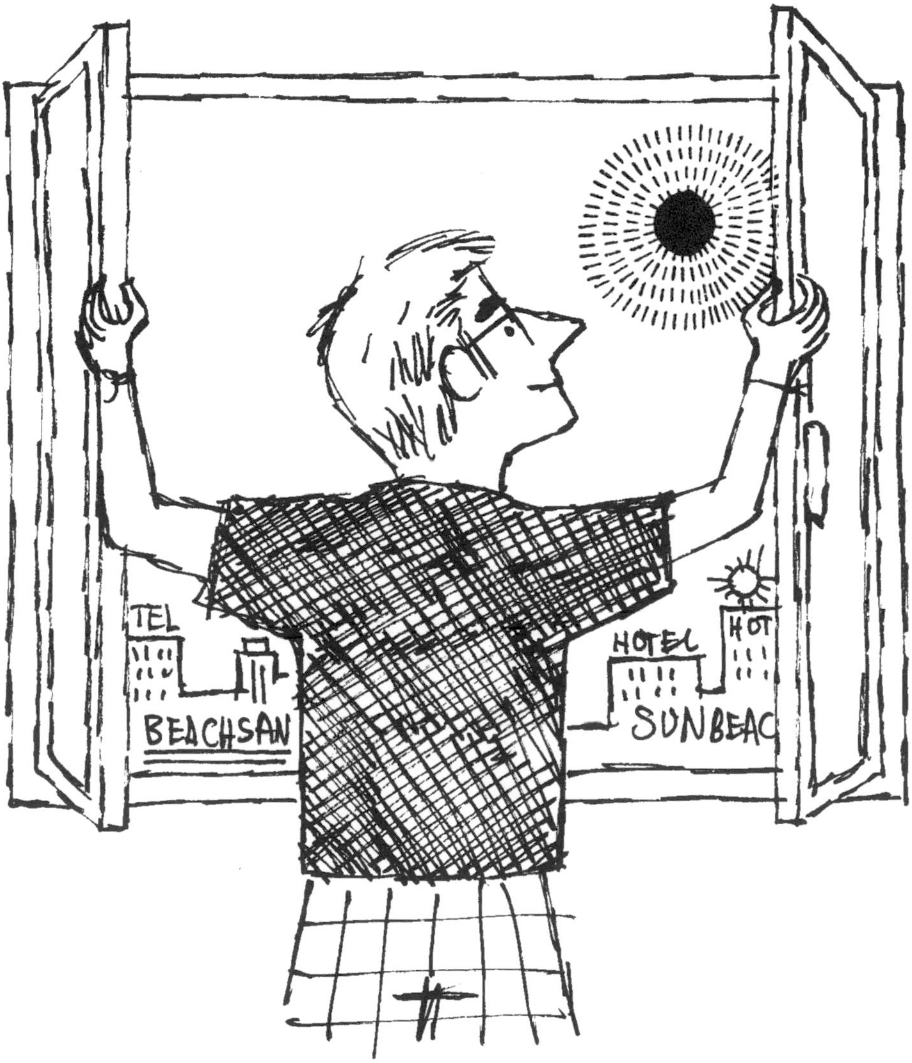
TEL
BEACHSAN
HOTEL
HOT
SUNBEAC

IT'S RAINING CATS AND DOGS ON THE MAINLAND – THE FLOATS IN THE HOLY WEEK PROCESSIONS ARE BEING ROWED THROUGH THE STREETS! EVERYONE IS LOOKING GLUMLY AT THE CLOUD-COVERED BEACHES. BUT NOT HERE! WE'VE GOT PLENTY OF SUN.

BESIDES, TODAY WE HAVE...AQUAGYM! DARTS! WATER POLO! BINGO! KARAOKE! AND RIFLE SHOOTING!!

DOWNTIME

SOMETIMES MARÍA GETS BORED WITH ALL THE REGULAR STUFF THAT'S HAPPENING IN HER LIFE: SCHOOL, THE PARK, EATING, THE BEACH AND VISITING PEOPLE AND PLACES. SHE DOESN'T READ OR WATCH TV MUCH, AND THERE ARE FEW THINGS THAT REALLY CATCH HER ATTENTION. THAT'S WHEN MARÍA GOES INTO HERSELF AND STARTS A DANCE WITH HER HANDS AND HER ARMS. SHE SOMETIMES HITS HERSELF ON THE CHIN OR ON THE SHOULDERS. THIS STIMMING✱ SEEMS TO FOLLOW SOME INNER RHYTHM AND IS DIFFICULT TO STOP UNLESS YOU CAN OFFER HER A DEFINITE ALTERNATIVE.

PUTS THE PALM OF ONE HAND OVER THE BACK OF THE OTHER

HITS HERSELF ON THE CHIN

BANGS HER HANDS TOGETHER LIKE THIS

PLAS PLAS

HITS HERSELF ON THE NECK

CLAPS

MAKES STRANGE MOVEMENTS WITH HER HAND

ALL OF THIS IS ACCOMPANIED BY A SCREECH THAT OTHER PEOPLE FIND VERY DISTURBING, BUT I'M USED TO IT.

✱ STIMMING: REPETITION OF AN ACTION IN A CONSTANT AND SEEMINGLY MEANINGLESS WAY.

A WALL SURROUNDS MARÍA

A WALL SEEMS TO SURROUND MARÍA WHEN PEOPLE COME ACROSS HER FOR THE FIRST TIME. IT'S A WALL OF FEAR OF THE UNKNOWN. NOBODY KNOWS WHAT TO DO OR HOW TO BEHAVE AT FIRST; HOWEVER, PEOPLE WHO GET TO KNOW MARÍA, EVEN BRIEFLY, ARE ENCHANTED TO FIND THAT THE WALL THEY'D BUILT UP IS NOT THAT HIGH. IT'S TRUE THAT MARÍA IS VERY SENSITIVE TO REJECTION, AND SHE'LL ONLY GET CLOSE TO THOSE WHO ARE PREPARED TO PAY ATTENTION TO HER AND LISTEN TO HER. BUT I'VE KNOWN PEOPLE FALL IN LOVE WITH MARÍA AFTER HAVING ONLY SPOKEN WITH HER FOR A LITTLE WHILE AND REALIZED IT ISN'T THAT DIFFICULT TO COMMUNICATE.

MARÍA IS DIRECT, HONEST AND SINCERE AND TRUSTS (ALMOST) EVERYONE, AND IF SHE SMILES AT YOU, WELL, YOU'VE GOT IT MADE. BUT BE CAREFUL, MY FRIENDS...MARÍA IS NOT FOR THE FAINTHEARTED. IF SHE DOESN'T LIKE YOU (OR IF SHE LIKES YOU A LOT)...

SHE'LL PINCH HARD!!

MARÍA DOESN'T HAVE NORMAL CONVERSATIONS; THEY ALWAYS FOLLOW CERTAIN RIGID FORMS THAT SHE LIKES TO STICK TO. ONE PART OF HER SPEECH IS MADE UP OF HER LISTS OF NAMES, WHICH ARE THE KEYS TO HER MEMORIES OF THINGS SHE HAS DONE. THEY ARE PERFECTLY STORED IN ORDERED BOXES. IT'S LIKE WHEN YOU REMEMBER A SPECIAL MOVIE AND THE PERSON YOU'RE WITH ALSO REMEMBERS: YOU BOTH SHARE AN EMOTION. IT WORKS LIKE THIS WITH MARÍA: THE NAMES SHE SAYS ARE CONNECTED TO HER MEMORIES. THEY ARE THE END OF A LONG PIECE OF STRING THAT CONNECTS HER TO A BIRTHDAY PARTY, TO HER CLASS AT SCHOOL, TO A PARTICULAR FAMILY. EACH MEMORY HAS ITS INTEGRAL PARTS. SHE NEVER FORGETS A SINGLE ONE. THAT IS MARÍA'S GIFT: AN EXTRAORDINARY MEMORY FOR PEOPLE. THE REST OF MARÍA'S SPEECH IS MADE UP OF SET PHRASES RELATED TO THE SITUATION.

HER SPECIALITY IS FAMILY LISTS: COUSINS, UNCLES AND AUNTS, FRIENDS AND THEN, TAKEN OUT FROM THE VERY BOTTOM OF ONE OF HER BOXES, THE NAME OF SOMEONE THAT EVEN YOU HAD FORGOTTEN ABOUT (NOT ALL THAT UNUSUAL IN MY CASE), FOLLOWED BY HER OVERJOYED EXPRESSION WHEN SHE SEES THAT YOU ARE AMAZED AT HER MEMORY. THIS, MY FRIENDS, IS GOLD. MOMENTS OF PRIDE WITH MARÍA ARE NOT MEASURED BY THE STANDARDS OF OTHER PARENTS, BUT ON A DIFFERENT SCALE. ANY ADVANCE, ANY SMILE IS A GREAT SOURCE OF JOY FOR THOSE AROUND MARÍA. AND MARÍA NEVER FAILS TO GIVE US REASONS TO REJOICE.

A TYPICAL CONVERSATION WITH MARÍA

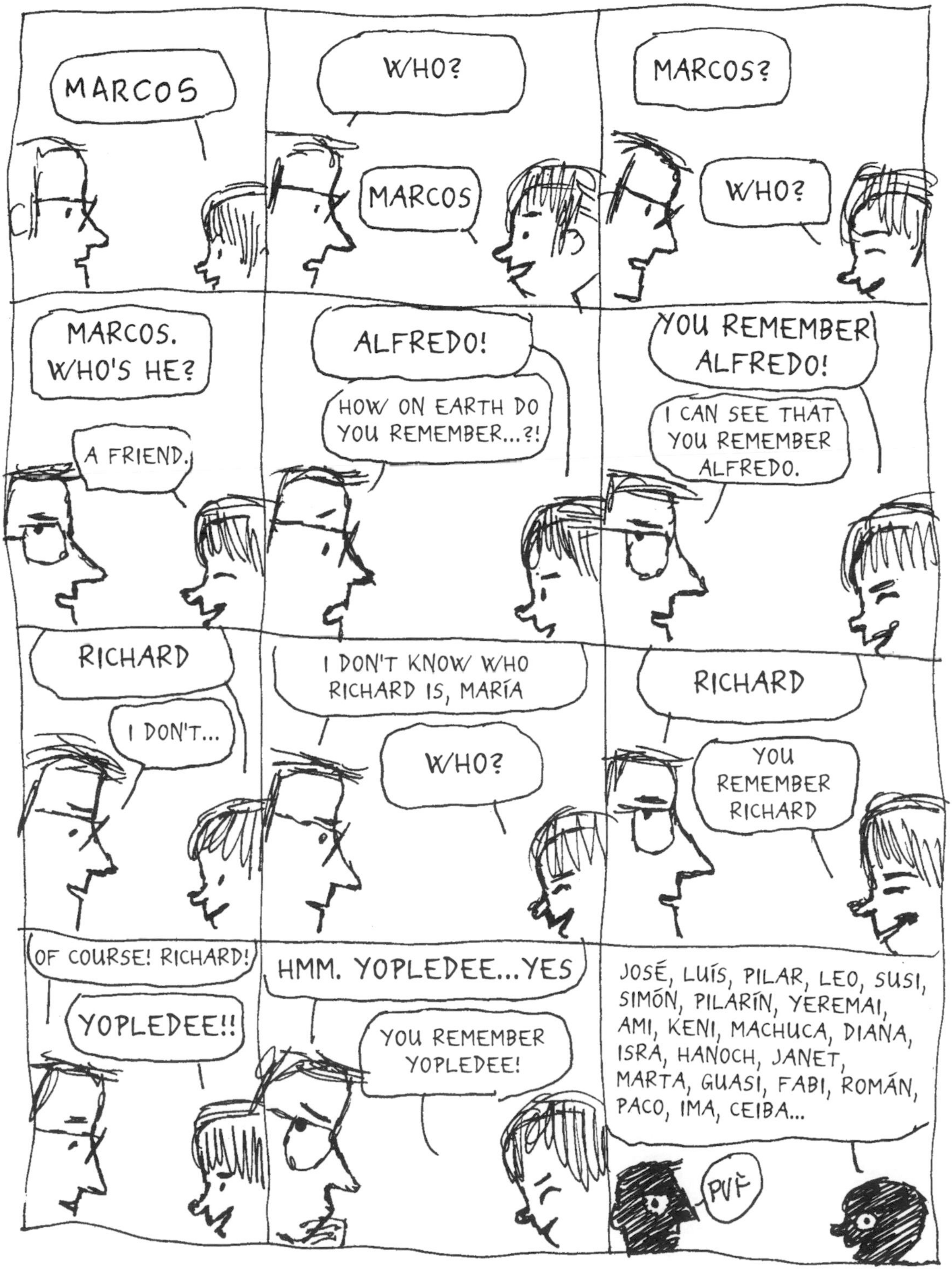

MARCOS
WHO?
MARCOS
MARCOS?
WHO?
MARCOS. WHO'S HE?
A FRIEND.
ALFREDO!
HOW ON EARTH DO YOU REMEMBER...?!
YOU REMEMBER ALFREDO!
I CAN SEE THAT YOU REMEMBER ALFREDO.
RICHARD
I DON'T...
I DON'T KNOW WHO RICHARD IS, MARÍA
WHO?
RICHARD
YOU REMEMBER RICHARD
OF COURSE! RICHARD!
YOPLEDEE!!
HMM. YOPLEDEE...YES
YOU REMEMBER YOPLEDEE!
JOSÉ, LUÍS, PILAR, LEO, SUSI, SIMÓN, PILARÍN, YEREMAI, AMI, KENI, MACHUCA, DIANA, ISRA, HANOCH, JANET, MARTA, GUASI, FABI, ROMÁN, PACO, IMA, CEIBA...
PUF

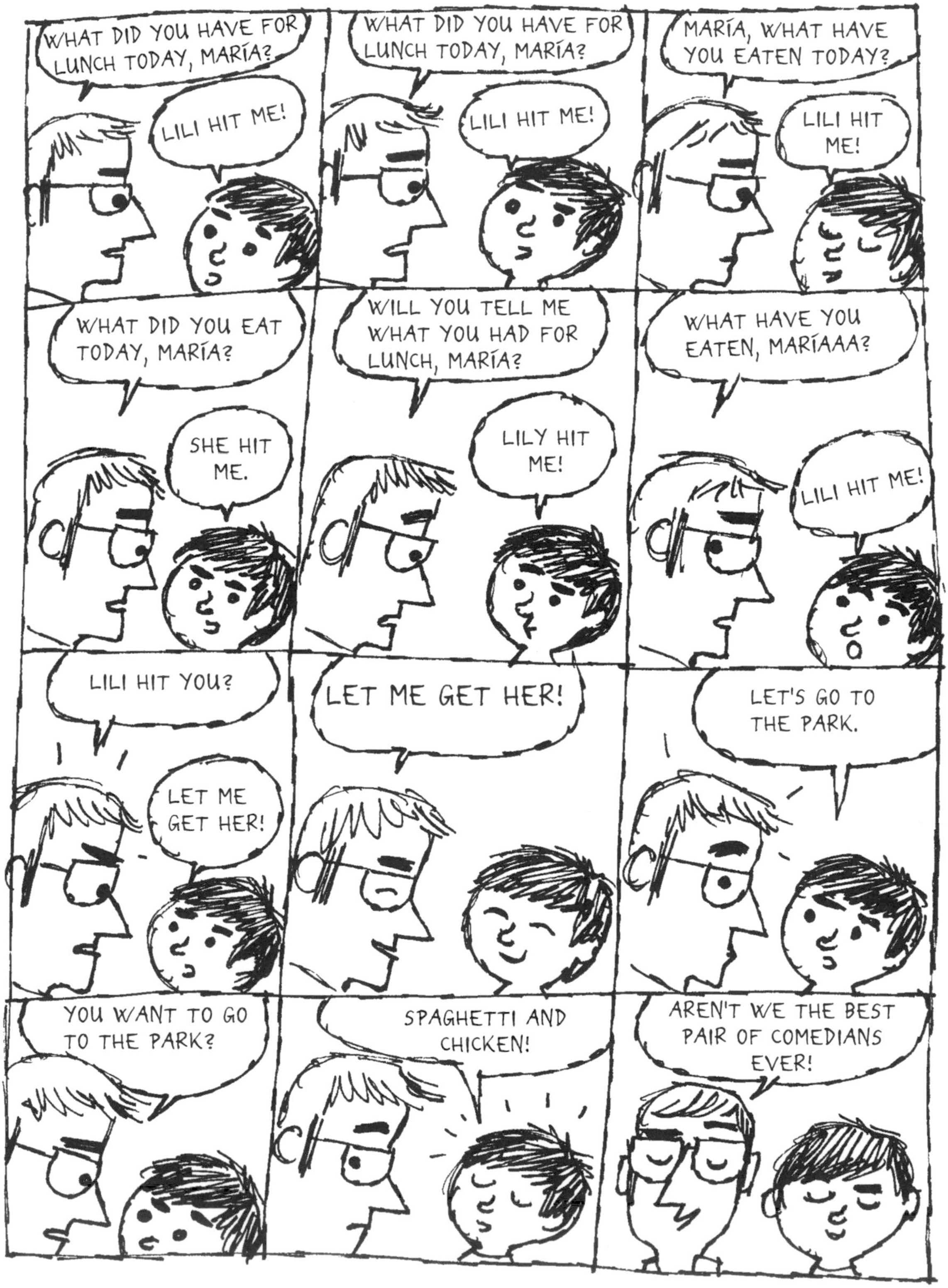
WHAT DID YOU HAVE FOR LUNCH TODAY, MARÍA?
LILI HIT ME!
WHAT DID YOU HAVE FOR LUNCH TODAY, MARÍA?
LILI HIT ME!
MARÍA, WHAT HAVE YOU EATEN TODAY?
LILI HIT ME!
WHAT DID YOU EAT TODAY, MARÍA?
SHE HIT ME.
WILL YOU TELL ME WHAT YOU HAD FOR LUNCH, MARÍA?
LILY HIT ME!
WHAT HAVE YOU EATEN, MARÍAAA?
LILI HIT ME!
LILI HIT YOU?
LET ME GET HER!
LET ME GET HER!
LET'S GO TO THE PARK.
YOU WANT TO GO TO THE PARK?
SPAGHETTI AND CHICKEN!
AREN'T WE THE BEST PAIR OF COMEDIANS EVER!

YESTERDAY MARÍA PUT ON HER SOCKS USING BOTH HANDS!

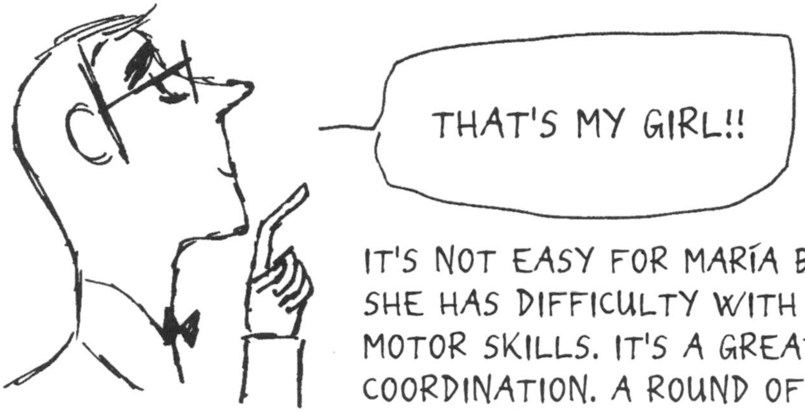
THAT'S MY GIRL!!

IT'S NOT EASY FOR MARÍA BECAUSE SHE HAS DIFFICULTY WITH FINE MOTOR SKILLS. IT'S A GREAT FEAT OF COORDINATION. A ROUND OF APPLAUSE FOR MARÍA!

TODAY IS SUNDAY, OUR LAST DAY IN THE TROPICAL PARADISE THAT IS DORADO BEACH.

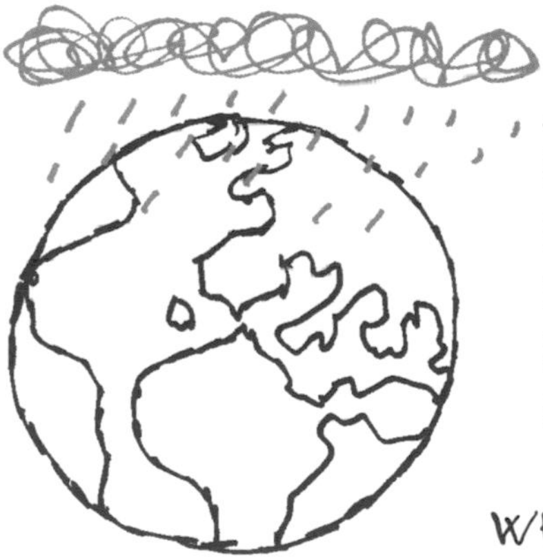

ACCORDING TO THE WEATHER REPORTS, IT'S BEEN RAINING HEAVILY ALL NIGHT JUST A FEW KILOMETRES FROM HERE, BUT HERE IT'S ANOTHER LOVELY SUNNY DAY.

WE'RE LUCKY, MARÍA AND ME!

BEFORE WE WENT TO SLEEP YESTERDAY, AFTER OUR ESCAPADE TO THE GREAT MANDARIN CHINESE RESTAURANT TO STUFF OURSELVES WITH FRIED RICE AND SHRIMP, MARÍA SNUGGLED UP TO ME AND SAID YOU AND ME... AS SIMPLE AS THAT. I HAD NEVER HEARD WORDS OF AFFECTION SO BEAUTIFUL AND SO SIMPLE.

THE PERFECT BEACH

IT'S OUR LAST DAY ON THE BEACH AT ANFI IN THE SOUTH OF THE ISLAND OF GRAN CANARIA. TODAY WE'VE BEEN ALONE FOR A LONG WHILE ON THIS BEACH OF WHITE SAND (SHELL DUST FROM SOME FARAWAY LAND) WITH CLEAR BLUE WATER THAT REMINDS YOU OF THE CARIBBEAN PICTURES YOU SEE IN GUIDE BOOKS. AFTER OUR AFTERNOON SNACK, I GO TO THE TRASH CAN AT THE FAR END OF THE BEACH.

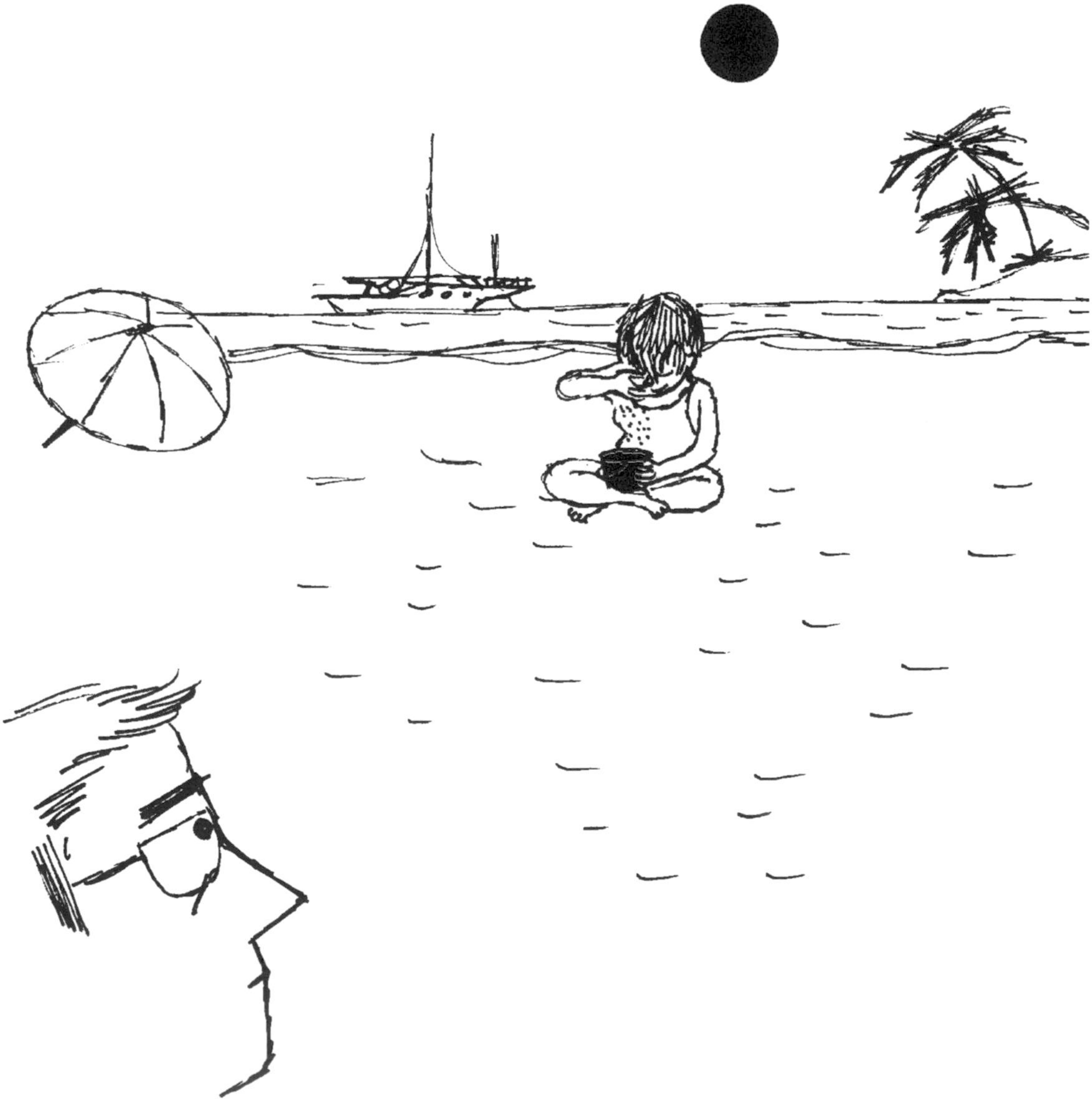

AS I LOOK BACK, I SEE MARÍA, SMALL IN THE MIDDLE OF THE EMPTY BEACH, ALONE AND PLAYING WITH HER PRECIOUS SAND. I FEEL SAD TO SEE HER OVER THERE, AND THINK ABOUT THE REST OF US – HOW WE GET CLOSE TO HER AND THEN LEAVE HER TO GET ON WITH HER OWN THING. I WISH FOR HER PARADISE TO BE SOMEWHERE SHE CAN ESCAPE TO SOMETIMES: SOMEWHERE LIKE THIS – A NEVER-ENDING BEACH OF FINE SAND, WITH A BLUE HORIZON, A SUN THAT NEVER SETS AND A RED BUCKET. PEOPLE ARE WITH HER AND THEN WE DISAPPEAR (AT LEAST THAT'S THE IMPRESSION WE GIVE HER, NEVER APPEARING TO MISS ANYONE WHEN WE LEAVE). IF ONLY THIS PERFECT BEACH COULD ALWAYS BE WITH HER, AND IF ONLY MARÍA'S SAND COULD NEVER RUN OUT.

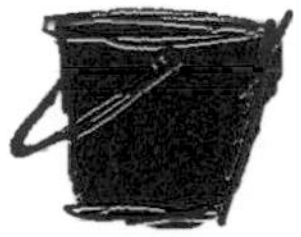

THE MORNING OF OUR DEPARTURE, JUST AS WE ARE TAKING ADVANTAGE OF OUR LAST MOMENTS BY THE POOL, A BIG STORM BREAKS, BUT EVEN THEN THE SUN IS STILL SHINING. SURPRISING AND LOVELY.

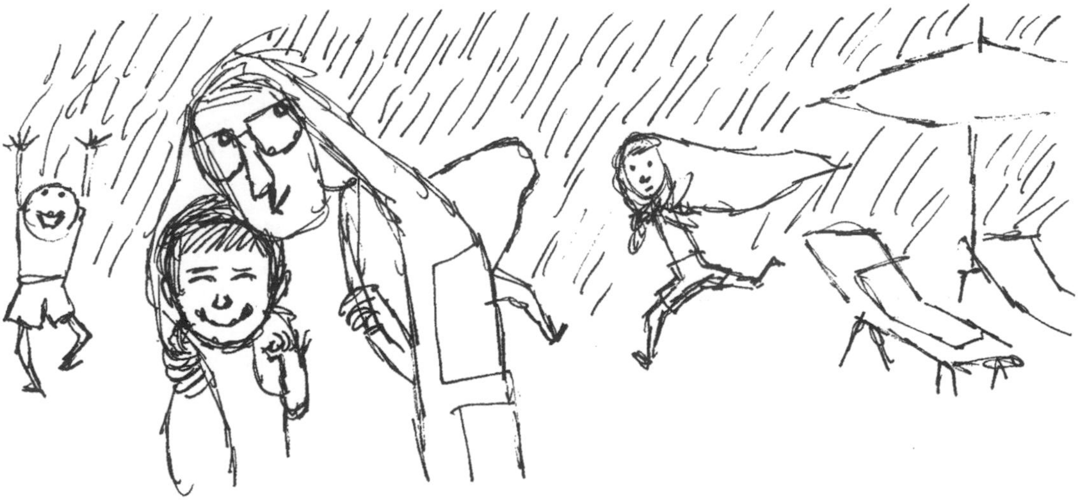

AT MIDDAY MARÍA'S MOTHER, MAY, COMES TO COLLECT US TO TAKE US TO HER HOUSE.

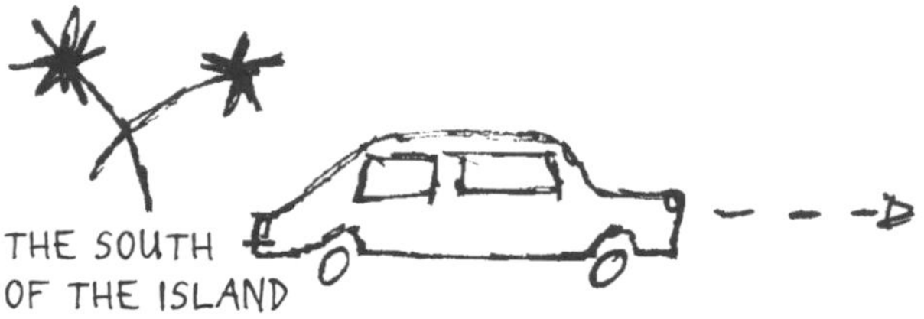
THE SOUTH
OF THE ISLAND

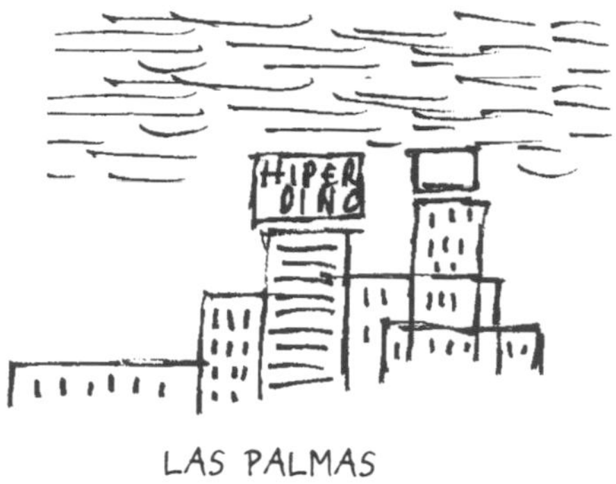
HIPER DINO
LAS PALMAS

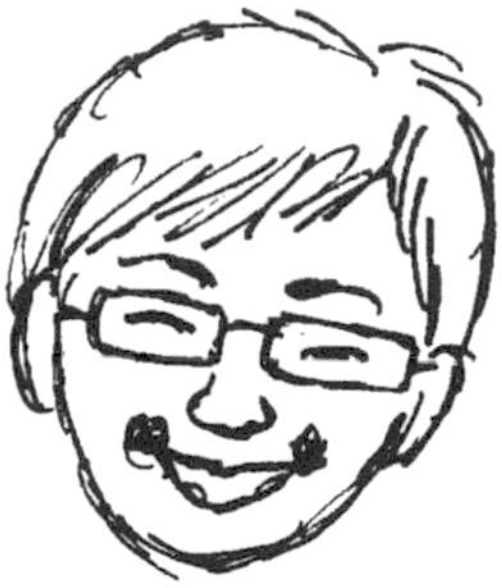
MAY

MARÍA LIVES WITH MAY AND HER GRANDFATHER PEPE, WHO I THINK IS HER FAVORITE PERSON IN THE WORLD.

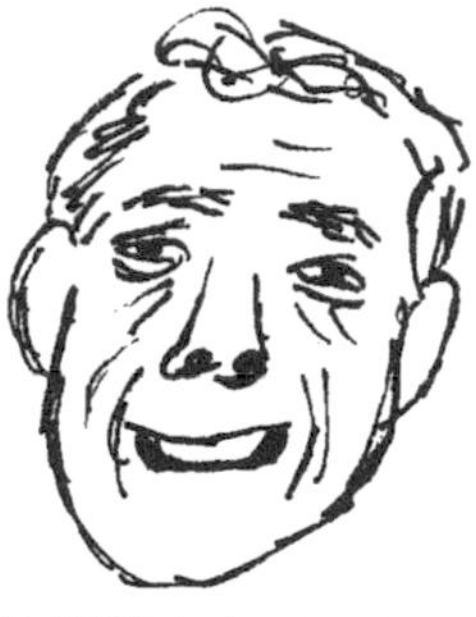
GRANDPA PEPE

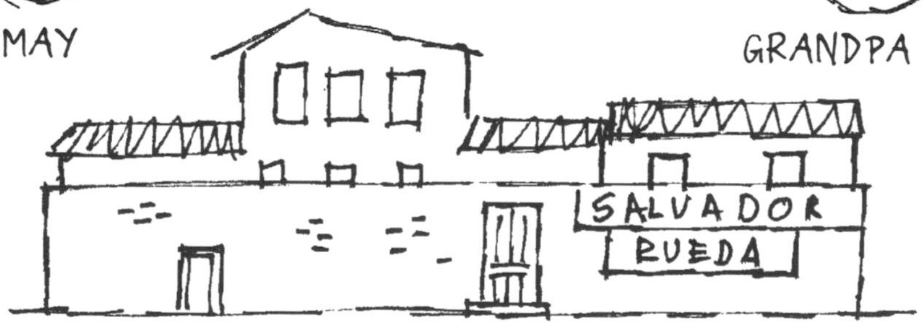
SALVADOR
RUEDA

IN THE AFTERNOON I TAKE MARÍA TO HER SCHOOL FOR A SWIMMING LESSON. TODAY SHE WILL SEE SOME OF HER BEST FRIENDS.

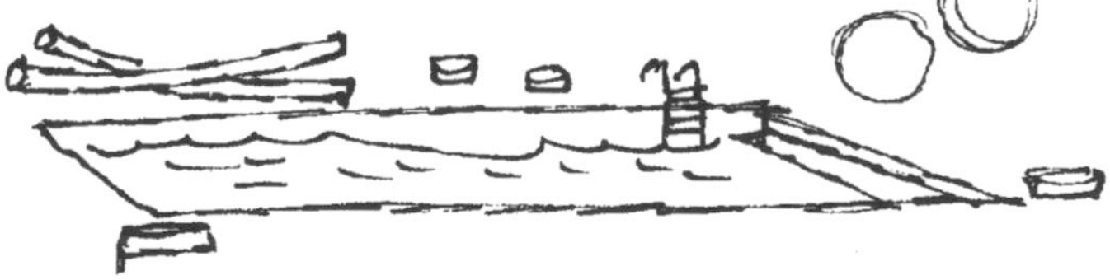

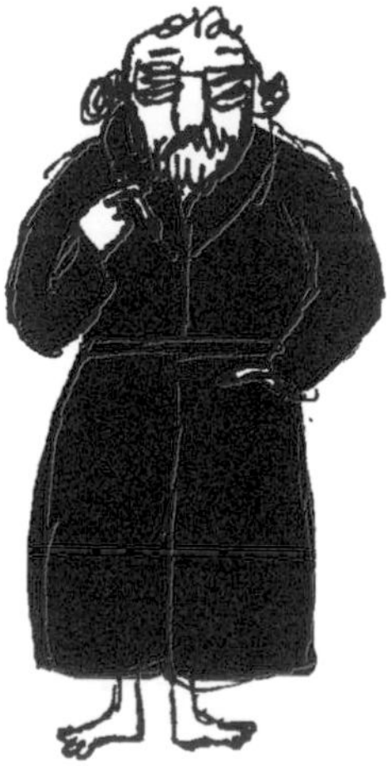

HER INSTRUCTOR IS ROMÁN, A GENTLE GIANT AND A BIT OF A HIPPY, WHO HAS TURNED A SMALL SWIMMING POOL INTO A DIFFERENT WORLD WHERE CHILDREN FEEL SAFE AND HAPPY.

ROMÁN IN BATHROBE

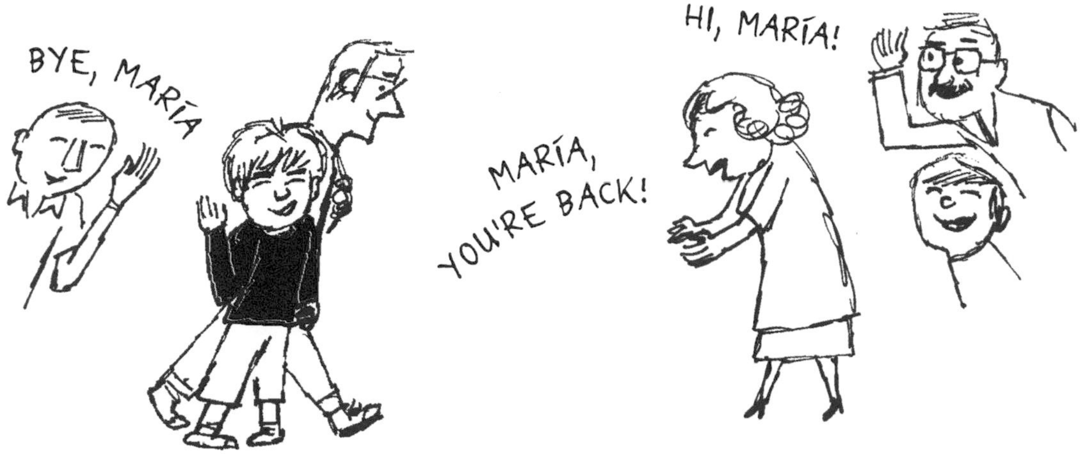
BYE, MARÍA
MARÍA, YOU'RE BACK!
HI, MARÍA!

ON THE WAY BACK HOME, AS WE GET CLOSE TO MARÍA'S NEIGHBORHOOD, I CAN SEE HOW MUCH PEOPLE LIKE MARÍA. EVERYONE WANTS HER TO GIVE THEM ONE OF HER SMILES OR FOR HER TO REMEMBER THEIR NAMES.

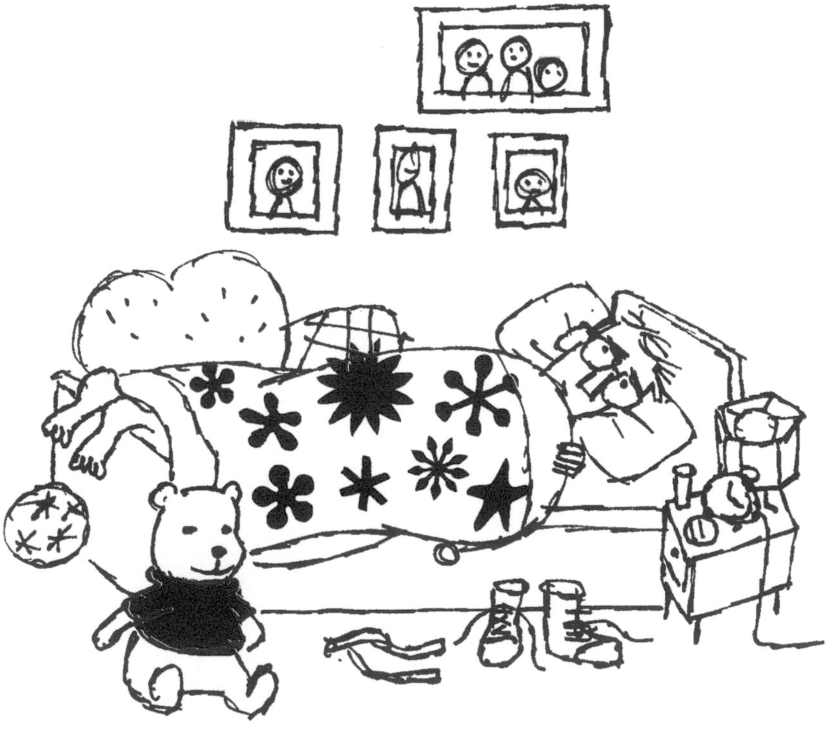

AT NIGHT I SLEEP IN MARÍA'S BED. IT'S SAD BUT NICE AT THE SAME TIME. IT SMELLS OF HER AND HER THINGS ARE ALL AROUND.

HELLO AND GOODBYE

MARÍA'S ROOM IS LIKE A WALK THROUGH HER LIFE. THERE
ARE HER TEDDY BEARS FROM WHEN SHE WAS SMALL, HER
FAVORITE STORY BOOKS (ALTHOUGH SHE DOESN'T READ
THEM, SHE ENJOYS GETTING THEM OUT SOMETIMES), A
BARBIE AND OTHER PLASTIC DOLLS, WINNIE THE POOH,
CHICKENS, TURTLES, RECORDS BY JUANES AND PAULINA
RUBIO...AND, DOMINATING EVERYTHING, IN THE MIDDLE OF
THE CARPET, A HUGE PILE OF PHOTOGRAPHS AND DRAWINGS
OF PEOPLE THAT I'VE MADE OVER THE YEARS. THESE ARE
THE PICTURES SHE LOOKS AT OVER AND OVER AGAIN, THAT
SHE CLASSIFIES AND PUTS IN ORDER, THAT SHE SEPARATES
AND CHOOSES. THERE, THE PEOPLE DON'T MOVE, THEY DON'T
DISAPPEAR, THEY DON'T GO ANYWHERE AND THEY DON'T
CHANGE. THEY MAKE THE WORLD A SAFER PLACE. I GET
SLEEPY LOOKING AT SOME PHOTOS THAT ARE ALSO MINE, OF
MY LIFE... I'M FALLING ASLEEP.

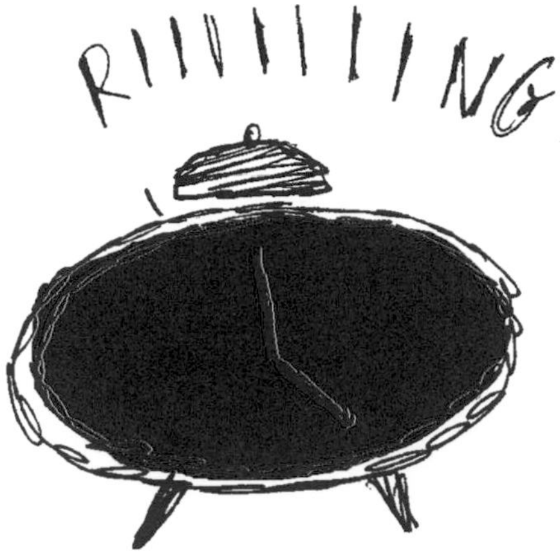
RIIIIIIIING

OHHH! ... THE ALARM GOES OFF AT FIVE IN THE MORNING. I HAVE TO GET UP... MY FLIGHT BACK TO BARCELONA LEAVES AT SEVEN.

CANARIES, MAY 2007

CAST

FOR YEARS I HAVE BEEN DRAWING FOR MARÍA IN NOTEBOOKS, ON LOOSE SHEETS AND ON WRAPPING PAPER. I'VE DRAWN ALL THE GROUPS OF PEOPLE THAT SHE CARES ABOUT AND LIKES — RELATIVES, KIDS FROM SCHOOL, FRIENDS... THESE ARE JUST SOME OF THE DRAWINGS OF THOSE PEOPLE AT BIRTHDAYS OR OTHER OCCASIONS. MARÍA RECOGNIZES THE PEOPLE AND ENJOYS NAMING THEM OVER AND OVER.

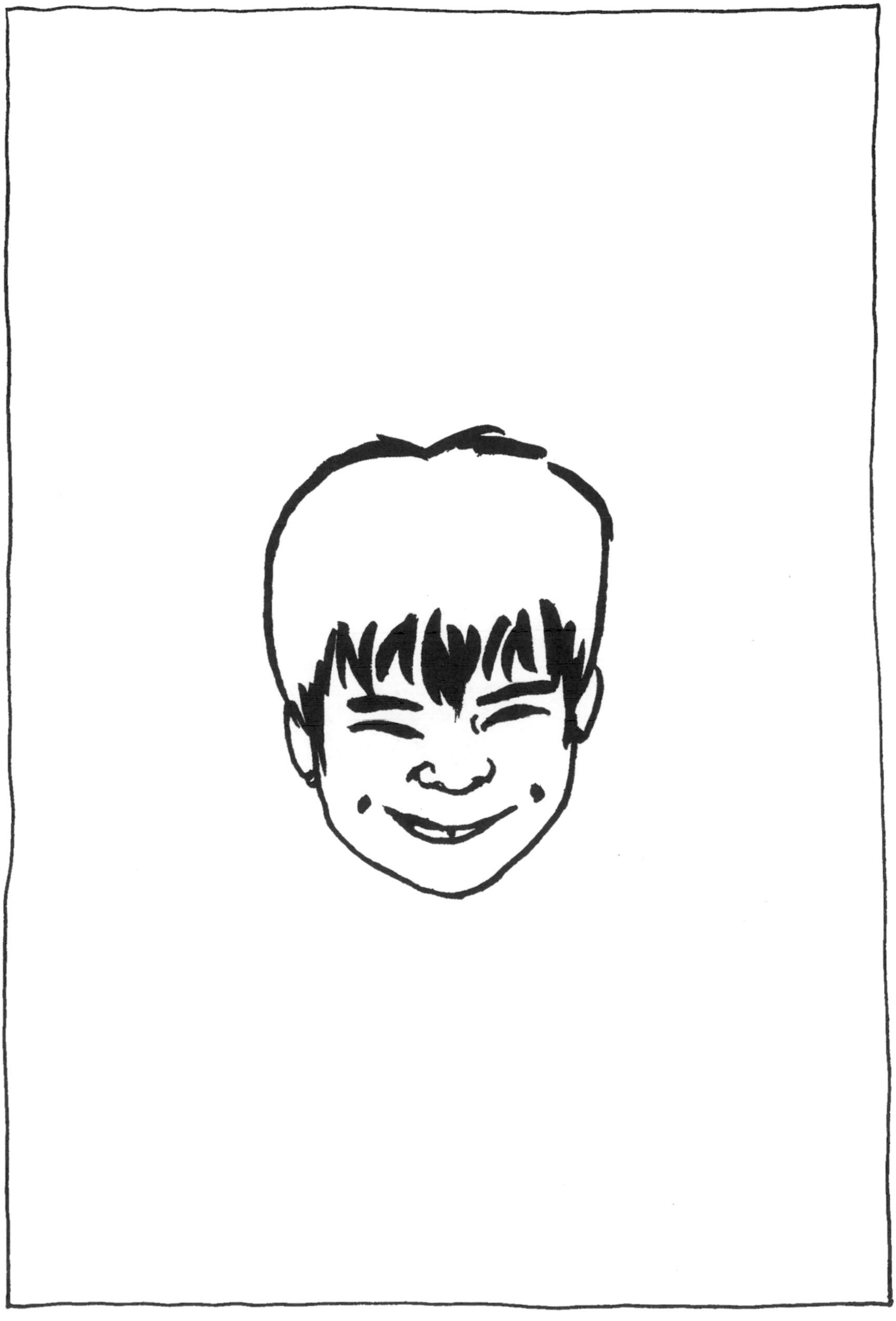

CAST IN THE CANARIES

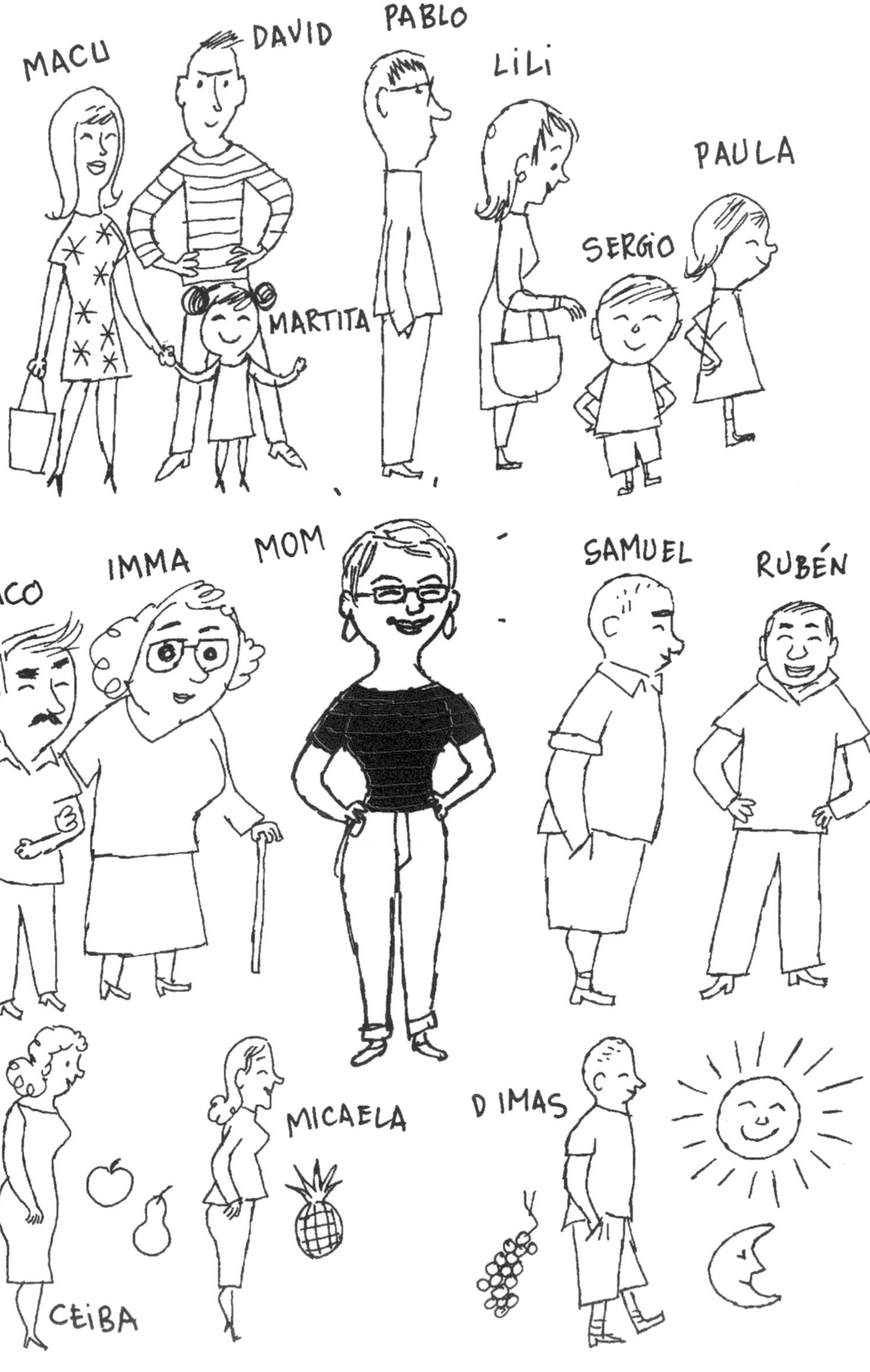
MACU
DAVID
PABLO
LILI
PAULA
SERGIO
MARTITA
PACO
IMMA
MOM
SAMUEL
RUBÉN
MICAELA
DIMAS
CEIBA

CAST IN THE CANARIES II

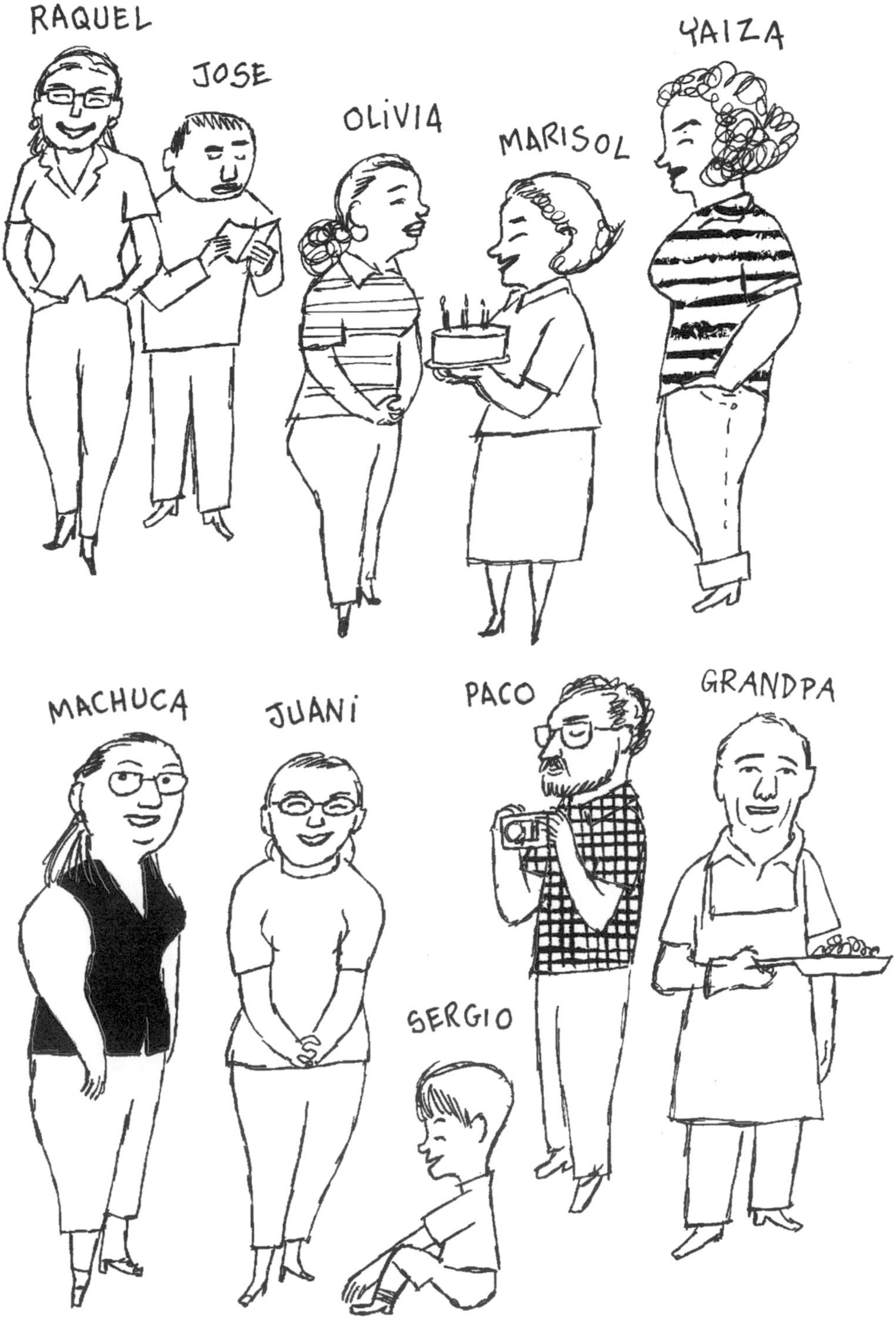
RAQUEL
JOSE
OLIVIA
MARISOL
YAIZA
MACHUCA
JUANI
PACO
GRANDPA
SERGIO

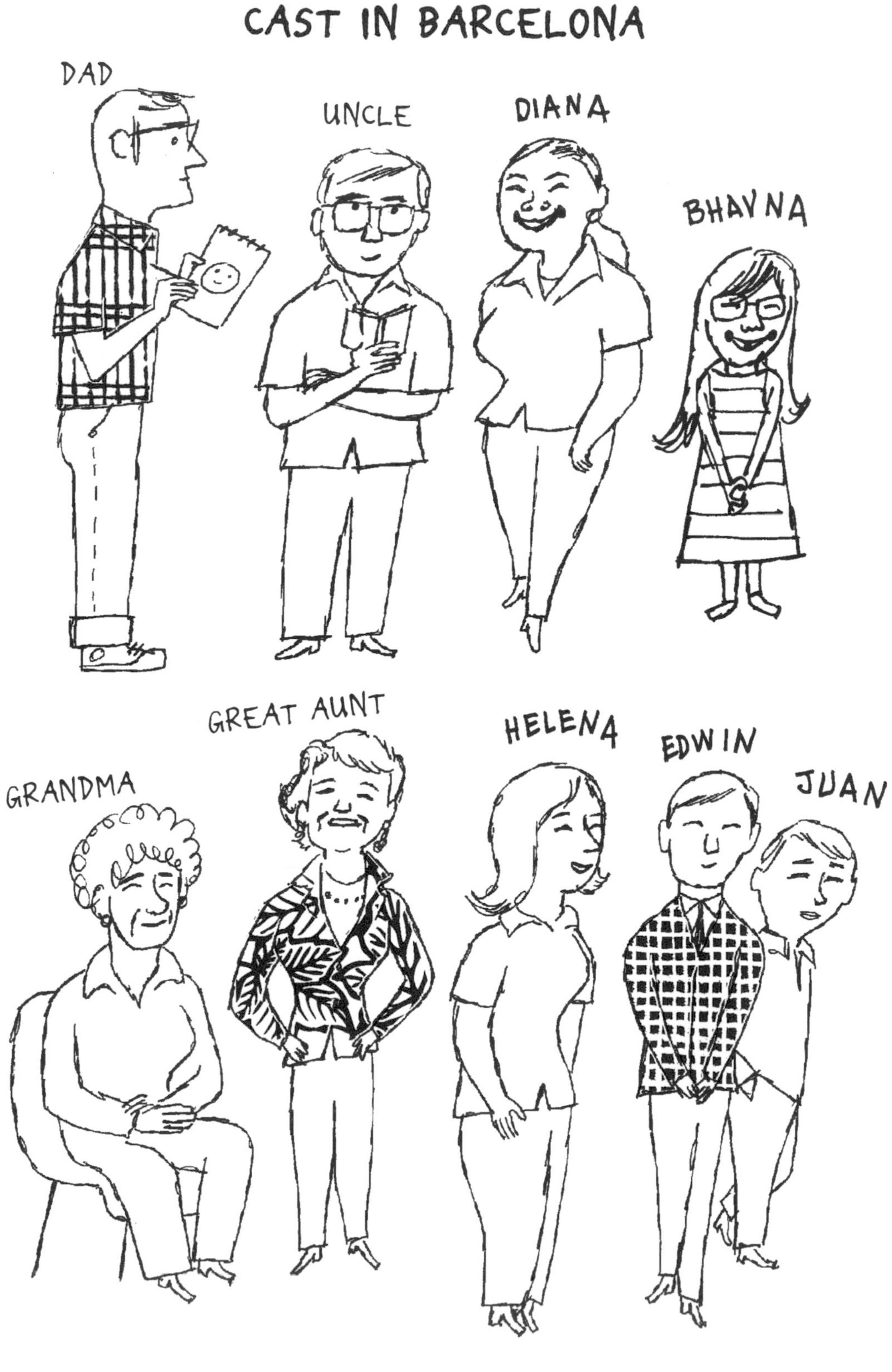
CAST IN BARCELONA
DAD
UNCLE
DIANA
BHAVNA
GREAT AUNT
GRANDMA
HELENA
EDWIN
JUAN

WHO CAME TO THE SUMMER'S END PARTY?

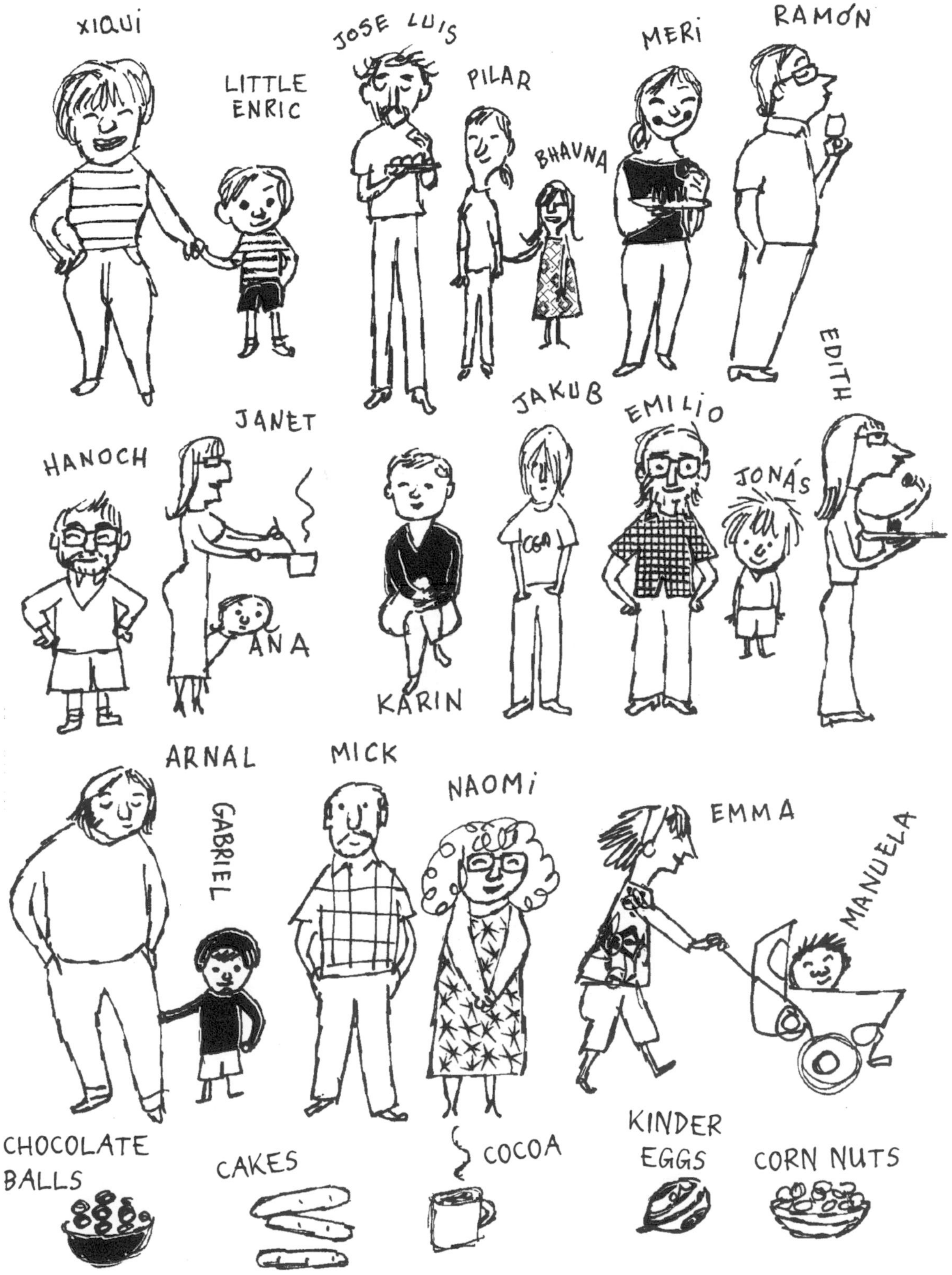
XIQUI
LITTLE ENRIC
JOSE LUIS
PILAR
BHAVNA
MERI
RAMÓN
EDITH
HANOCH
JANET
JAKUB
EMILIO
JONÁS
ANA
KARIN
ARNAL
GABRIEL
MICK
NAOMI
EMMA
MANUELA
CHOCOLATE BALLS
CAKES
COCOA
KINDER EGGS
CORN NUTS

WHO WAS AT THE NEW YEAR'S DINNER?

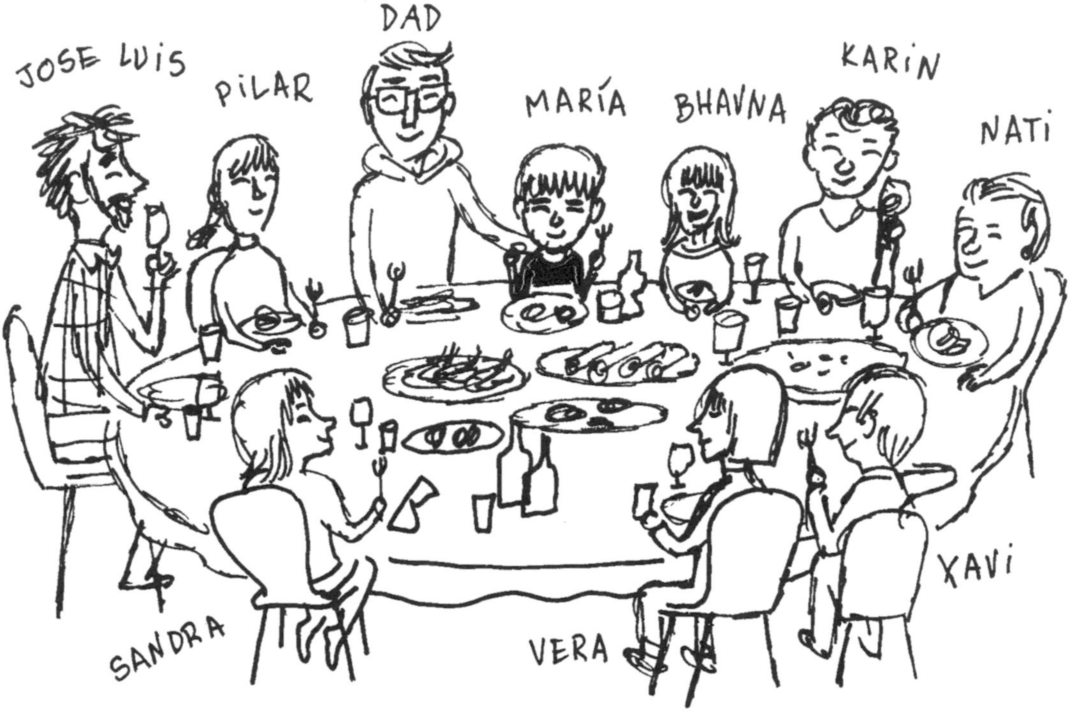
JOSE LUIS
PILAR
DAD
MARÍA
BHAVNA
KARIN
NATI
SANDRA
VERA
XAVI

WHO COULDN'T COME TO THE MEAL BUT TURNED UP LATER?

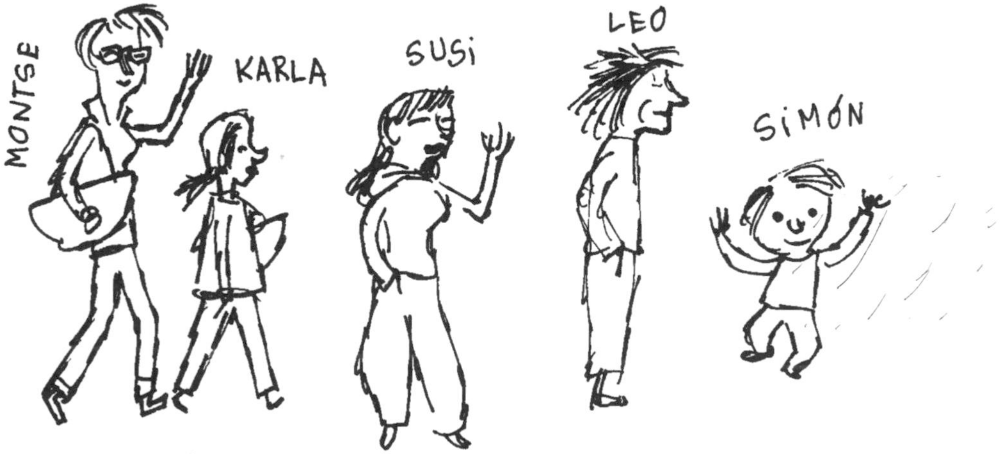
MONTSE
KARLA
SUSI
LEO
SIMÓN

MARTA, BAXTER, HELÈNE, BIEL, BALO, SILVIA, BIEL II, SEÑOR JUAN, ANA, JORGE, FÉLIX AND HIS TRUMPET, BOJÁN & DANE & LUCAS, PABLO, CAMILA & SONIA & DARIO & PINI AND MANY MORE ALSO CAME JUST TO SAY GOODBYE TO MARÍA UNTIL NEXT YEAR.

MARÍA'S CHORES

THESE ARE SOME OF THE PICTOGRAMS THAT MARÍA USES. CHILDREN WITH AUTISM ARE GOOD AT PROCESSING INFORMATION VISUALLY, BUT THEY HAVE PROBLEMS ANTICIPATING WHAT IS LIKELY TO HAPPEN, AND THIS CAUSES STRESS AND FRUSTRATION. PICTOGRAMS ALLOW FOR ACTIVITIES TO BE STRUCTURED AND PLANNED. PLACED ALL AROUND THE HOME, THEY HELP MARÍA TO ANTICIPATE WHAT IS GOING TO HAPPEN DURING THE DAY.

WHAT HAPPENS WHEN YOU GO TO THE TOILET?

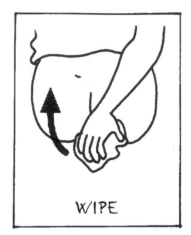

LIFT THE LID

SIT DOWN

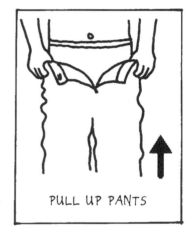

WIPE

THROW AWAY
THE PAPER

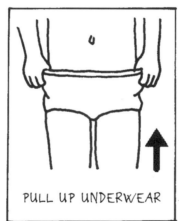

PULL UP UNDERWEAR

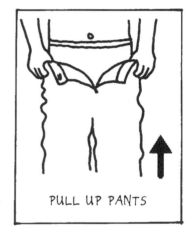

PULL UP PANTS

TURN ON FAUCET

WASH HANDS

TURN OFF FAUCET

WEDNESDAY'S SCHEDULE

GET DRESSED

LEAVE HOME

GO TO SCHOOL

COME BACK HOME

PLAY

HAVE A SHOWER

HAVE DINNER

WATCH TV

GO TO SLEEP

AND THAT'S IT. MARÍA
IS MARÍA AND I AM HER
DAD. SOMETIMES WE GET
MAD AT EACH OTHER
BUT MORE OFTEN WE
LAUGH. WE NEVER STOP
TALKING, ESPECIALLY
MARÍA. I LIKE DRAWING
FOR HER AND THAT'S
A WAY FOR US TO
COMMUNICATE WITH
EACH OTHER. MARÍA IS
THE BEST DAUGHTER
THAT ANY FATHER
COULD WISH FOR.

THIS IS ONE OF THE
FIRST DRAWINGS I MADE
OF MARÍA, PULLING ME
AS ALWAYS. A REAL
CHARACTER.

AUTISM

PEOPLE WITH AUTISM CAN EXHIBIT THE FOLLOWING CHARACTERISTICS, IN DIFFERENT COMBINATIONS AND WITH DIFFERENT LEVELS OF SEVERITY.

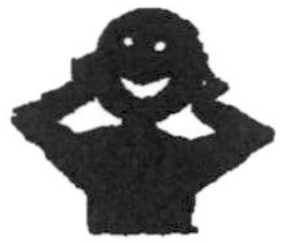

LAUGHING AT INAPPROPRIATE MOMENTS

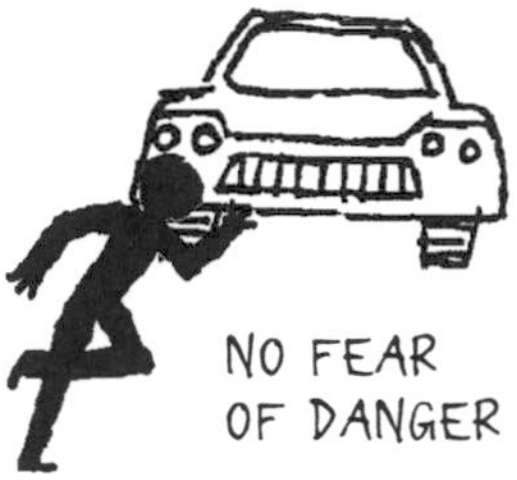

NO FEAR OF DANGER

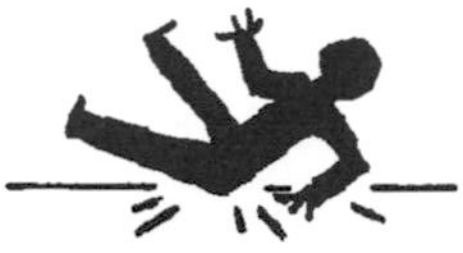

APPARENT INSENSIBILITY TO PAIN

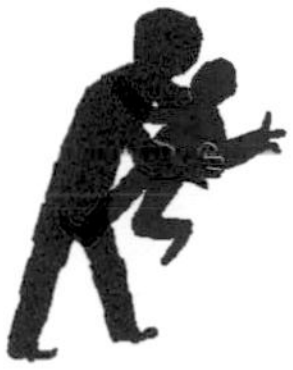

THEY CAN REJECT AFFECTION

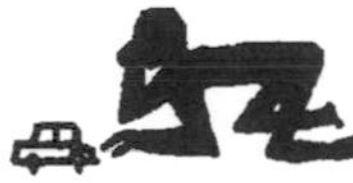

OBSESSIVE DEDICATION TO UNUSUAL OR REPETITIVE GAMES

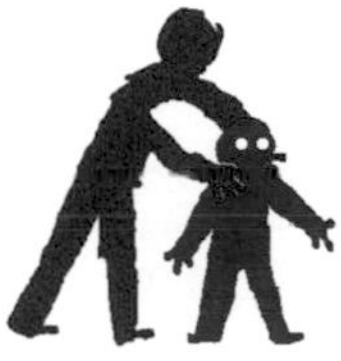

THEY MAY AVOID EYE CONTACT

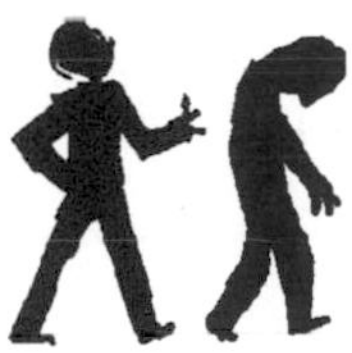

THEY MAY PREFER TO BE ALONE

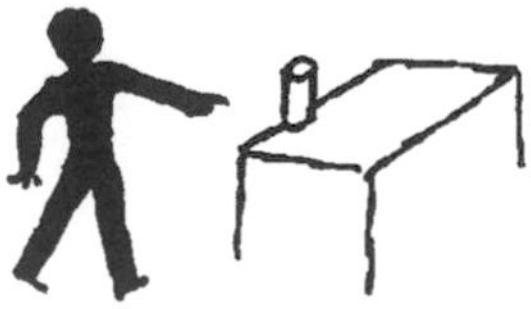

DIFFICULTY EXPRESSING THEIR NEEDS, RESORTING TO GESTURES

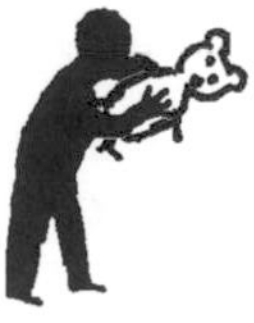

INAPPROPRIATE ATTACHMENT TO OBJECTS

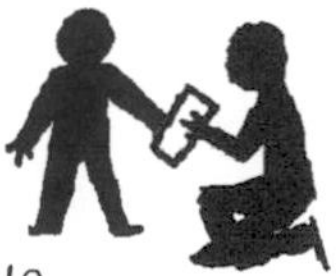

BEING OVER-INSISTENT

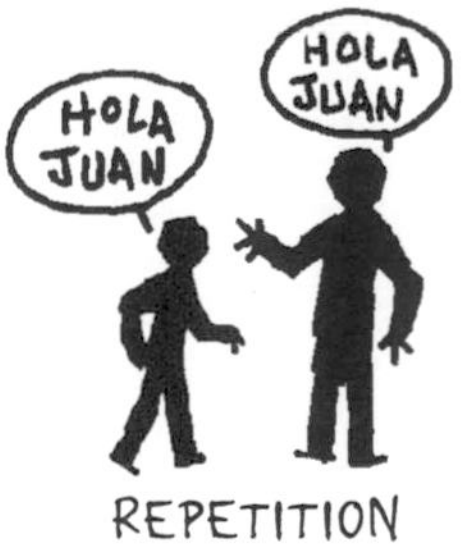
HOLA JUAN
HOLA JUAN

REPETITION OF WORDS AND PHRASES

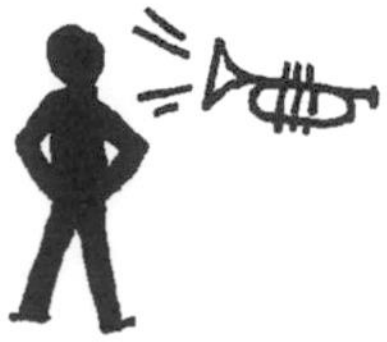

EXTREME LACK OF REACTION OR RESPONSE TO SOUNDS

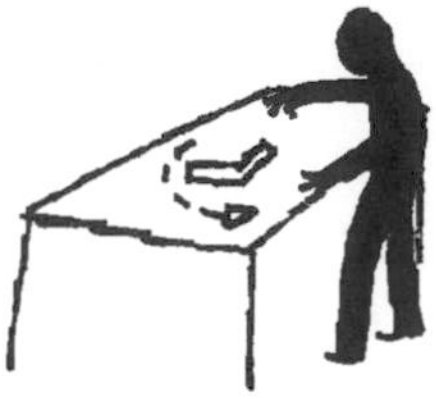

SPINNING THEMSELVES AROUND OR TURNING OBJECTS AROUND

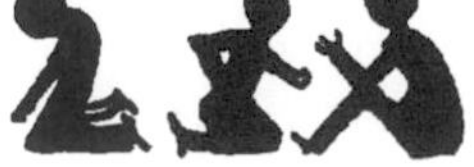

DIFFICULTY INTERACTING WITH OTHERS

ACKNOWLEDGMENTS

TO DAIDA WHO HELPED ME WITH THE PICTOGRAMS, VANESA
WHO TAKES MARÍA TO THE SCHOOL BUS EVERY DAY, CEIBA,
MARÍA'S FAVORITE COUSIN, HANOCH WHO ENCOURAGED
ME, SERGIO, MARTITA, BRUNO, PAULA AND ALL OF MARÍA'S
COUSINS WHO ENSURE SHE HAS A BIRTHDAY EVERY WEEK.
TO ASTIBERRI WHO MAKES SOME BEAUTIFUL BOOKS, ILLIO
WHO MARÍA STILL REMEMBERS AFTER ONLY HAVING SEEN HIM
ONCE IN THE PARK FOUR YEARS AGO. TO PAQUI, TITA, SONIA
AND ALL OF MARÍA'S TEACHERS, ROMÁN, TO THE GROUND
STAFF OF I DON'T REMEMBER WHICH AIRLINE WHO SAVED US
FROM HAVING TO LINE UP TO BOARD. TO PILAR, MY AUNT, FOR
LETTING HERSELF BE PINCHED FROM TIME TO TIME. TO NATI
FOR ALWAYS GIVING MARÍA THREE HELPINGS OF PAELLA. TO
BHAVNA FOR PLAYING WITH MARÍA, TO MARTA FOR TALKING
TO HER WITHOUT KNOWING HER, TO IMA, PACO, MANUEL,
SENSA, MARU AND SARA FOR BELIEVING IN THE BOOK BEFORE
EVEN SEEING IT. TO ANGELS FOR SINGING TO HER, AND TO
YANKO AND BRIAN. TO AMAYA HERVÁS FOR HER PATIENCE.
TO WALT DISNEY FOR SLEEPING BEAUTY AND WINNIE THE
POOH. TO XIQUI FOR MAKING MARÍA LAUGH. TO FABI. TO TATI,
NIL AND ALL MARÍA'S CLASSMATES FROM BARCELONA, TO
ESME, CRISTINA, REYES, YOLANDA AND EVA. TO ROSER. TO
PILAR FOR GIVING HER TIME AND AFFECTION. TO THE BUS
DRIVER WHO WAITED FOR US TO SIT DOWN. TO DIANA WHO
PREPARED FROZEN SPINACH LIKE NOBODY ELSE, TO HELENA
FOR GIVING MARÍA A BATH AND SINGING SOFTLY TO HER. TO
PINO AND GUASI, KENI, KEVIN, KILLIAN, PAULA, RENÉ, DAILOS,
AMI, MACHUCA AND JUANI. TO DIMAS AND MICAELA (WHO,
MARÍA TELLS ME, IS FROM ROMANIA). TO DIEGO FROM THE
NEIGHBORHOOD COPY SHOP WHO ONCE TOOK SOME PHOTOS OF
MARÍA DRESSED AS SNOW WHITE. TO SEÑORA ANTONIA WHO
ALWAYS SAYS SOMETHING NICE TO HER, TO MARICARMEN AND
SEÑOR JUAN. TO MARISOL AND YAIZA AND OLIVIA.

TO PILARÍN AND JOSÉ-LUÍS, WHO ARE LIKE FAMILY, FOR LOVING MARÍA JUST AS SHE IS. TO HER GRANDFATHER PACO WHO KNEW HER FOR ONLY THREE YEARS AND TO HER GRANDMOTHER BENI WHO WAS ABLE TO SPEND A LITTLE MORE TIME WITH HER. TO HER GREAT-GRANDMOTHER MARÍA FOR GIVING HER SUCH A BEAUTIFUL NAME. TO FRANCESC, ELISENDA, LALI, MARTA AND ORIOL. TO THE TAXI DRIVER WHO DIDN'T COMPLAIN WHEN MARÍA STARTED TO SCREAM. TO BAXTER AND HELÈNE AND BIEL. TO SILVIA AND TO MY MOTHER, WHO FINDS IT DIFFICULT TO UNDERSTAND MARÍA BUT NEVER STOPS TRYING. TO TERESA FOR HER HELP. TO LILI, OLITO, RAQUEL AND JOSÉ. TO MACU AND DAVID. TO THE NURSE AT THE HOSPITAL DEL MAR WHO PUT US IN A BETTER ROOM. TO ALL THE PARENTS WHO GAVE HELP WHEN WE NEEDED IT. TO JANET WHO MAKES A CHOCOLATE MILKSHAKE THAT MARÍA LOVES. TO SUSI AND LEO WHO INVITE US UP TO THE MOUNTAINS WHENEVER WE'RE IN BARCELONA, AND TO SIMÓN WHO PULLS MARÍA'S HAIR. TO CAMILA FOR ALL HER HELP THROUGHOUT THE BOOK. TO MARIATE FOR WHISTLING FOR MARÍA. TO PAUL KARASIC FOR WRITING A BEAUTIFUL BOOK THAT MOVED ME. TO THE GERMAN LADY FROM THE RESORT WHO SMILED AT MARÍA ALL THE TIME, AND TO KARIN WHO PUTS UP WITH ME AND SUPPORTS ME IN EVERYTHING I DO.

THANK YOU

MIGUEL GALLARDO LIVES AND WORKS IN BARCELONA. HE IS AN ILLUSTRATOR FOR THE NEWSPAPER "LA VANGUARDIA" AS WELL AS OTHER SPANISH AND INTERNATIONAL PUBLICATIONS SUCH AS "THE HERALD TRIBUNE" AND "THE NEW YORKER." HE HAS WON PRIZES AT THE BARCELONA COMIC FAIR AND A SERRA D'OR AWARD FOR "QUÉ LE PASA A ESTE NIÑO?" ("WHAT'S UP WITH THAT KID?"), A CHILDREN'S GUIDE TO DISABILITY. AS WELL AS BEING ONE OF THE CREATORS OF "MAKOKI," HE HAS PUBLISHED OTHER WORKS SUCH AS "PERICO CARAMBOLA," "TRES VIAJES" ("THREE JOURNEYS") AND "UN LARGO SILENCIO" ("A LONG SILENCE"), A GRAPHIC NOVEL ABOUT THE SPANISH CIVIL WAR.

MARÍA WAS BORN IN 1994 AND WAS 12 YEARS OLD WHEN THIS BOOK WAS WRITTEN. NOW 22, SHE STILL LIVES IN THE CANARY ISLANDS AND GOES TO AN ADULT EDUCATION CENTER. IN SUMMER WE NO LONGER GO TO A RESORT, BUT SPEND OUR HOLIDAYS IN THE COSTA BRAVA, NEAR WHERE I LIVE.

EPILOGUE

ONE VERY IMPORTANT ASPECT OF TEACHING CHILDREN WITH AUTISM, RECOGNIZED BY PARENTS, TEACHERS AND OTHER PROFESSIONALS, IS THE USE OF CLEAR IMAGES THAT TRANSMIT IDEAS OR SITUATIONS. IN THIS BOOK, MIGUEL GALLARDO, WHO IS USED TO COMMUNICATING VISUALLY WITH HIS DAUGHTER MARÍA, SHARES THIS WITH HIS READERS AS IF WE WERE HER; THROUGH HIS DRAWINGS WE CAN UNDERSTAND HIS BRIEF AND SIMPLE MESSAGE IN AN UNEQUIVOCAL WAY.

THIS BOOK CORRECTS MANY STEREOTYPES ABOUT CHILDREN WITH AUTISM, WHICH IS BEING DIAGNOSED MORE AND MORE FREQUENTLY. MARÍA IS NEITHER DISTANT NOR COLD, BUT EMOTIONAL AND AFFECTIONATE, CONTRARY TO THE EXPECTATIONS OF HER AUTISM. WE CAN MAKE MARÍA AND OTHER CHILDREN LIKE HER HAPPIER BY SIMPLY ACCEPTING THEM JUST AS THEY ARE: UNIQUE, LIKE EVERYONE ELSE.

AMAYA HERVÁS

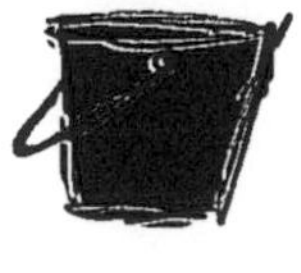

ENGLISH LANGUAGE EDITION FIRST PUBLISHED IN 2018
BY JESSICA KINGSLEY PUBLISHERS
73 COLLIER STREET
LONDON N1 9BE, UK
AND
400 MARKET STREET, SUITE 400
PHILADELPHIA, PA 19106, USA

WWW.JKP.COM

FIRST PUBLISHED IN SPANISH IN 2007 AS MARÍA Y YO BY ASTIBERRI PUBLISHERS, BILBAO, SPAIN

LIBRARY OF CONGRESS CATALOGING IN PUBLICATION DATA
A CIP CATALOG RECORD FOR THIS BOOK IS AVAILABLE FROM THE LIBRARY OF CONGRESS

BRITISH LIBRARY CATALOGUING IN PUBLICATION DATA
A CIP CATALOGUE RECORD FOR THIS BOOK IS AVAILABLE FROM THE BRITISH LIBRARY

ISBN 978 1 78592 381 4
EISBN 978 1 78450 729 9

PRINTED AND BOUND IN GREAT BRITAIN BY BELL & BAIN LTD, GLASGOW

MIX
Paper from
responsible sources
FSC® C007785
FSC
www.fsc.org